Strategies

for Building
Text-Dependent
Questions

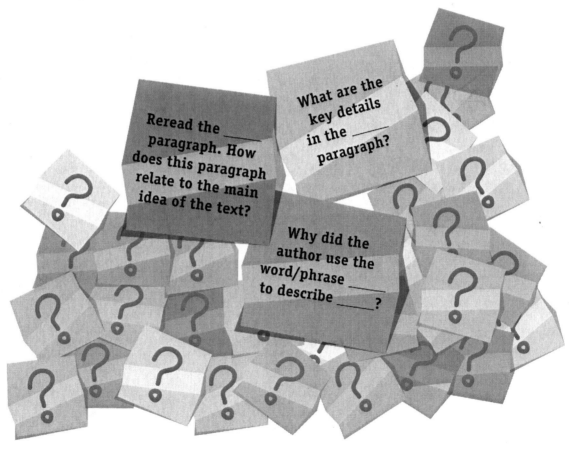

Reread the _____ paragraph. How does this paragraph relate to the main idea of the text?

What are the key details in the _____ paragraph?

Why did the author use the word/phrase _____ to describe _____?

Author

Jessica Hathaway

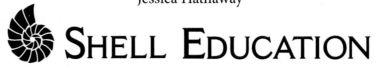

SHELL EDUCATION

Image Credits

p.44 US National Archives; p.51 William Henry Holmes, Origin & Development of Form and Ornament in Ceramic Art (2006) (p.448); p.78 Wikimedia Commons; p.100 patrickheagney/iStockphoto; p.176 Tomacco/iStockPhoto; p.208 Kropewnicki/iStockPhoto; p.228 LOC [LC-DIG-ggbain-30124]; p.263 Wikimedia Commons; p.265 LOC [LC-USP6-2415-A]; all other images Shutterstock

Standards

© 2010. National Governors Association Center for Best Practices and Council of Chief State School Officers. All rights reserved.

Shell Education

5301 Oceanus Drive
Huntington Beach, CA 92649-1030
http://www.shelleducation.com
ISBN 978-1-4258-1449-6
© 2014 Shell Educational Publishing, Inc.

Table of Contents

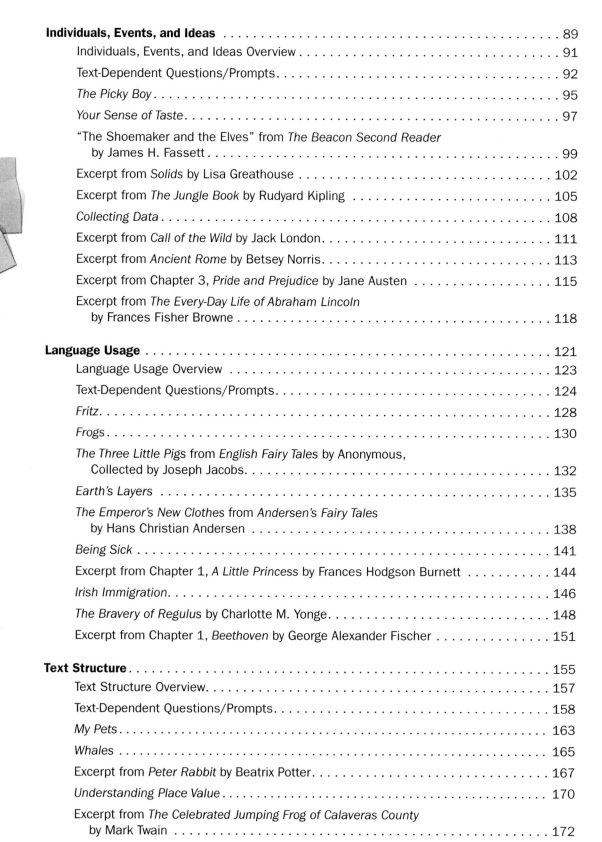

The Importance of Text-Dependent Questions

Curiosity is one of the fundamental human principles that drives the desire to learn. Starting at birth, we continuously wonder about the world around us. We question the information that we take in through our senses, analyzing and examining it so we can apply meaning to it. We strive to understand how things work, why things happen, and what things mean. We puzzle over mysteries of science, struggle to comprehend human psychology, and endeavor to solve great mathematical questions. It is this ability to question and doubt that propels us forward in our quest for knowledge and answers.

Within the realm of education, questions play an important role in helping teachers advance students' learning and comprehension. Teachers use questions to engage students' interest and motivate their learning. Questions help teachers focus the attention of their students on particular points and guide students' course of study. In school, questions can be used to highlight connections between materials in different content areas and help students draw conclusions based on their learning. They stimulate discussions and facilitate group learning. Finally, questions allow teachers to assess their students' progress and comprehension through a variety of different formats that range from standard multiple-choice tests to Socratic seminars.

Questions serve a variety of purposes and therefore, have a multitude of outcomes. While some questions simply demand students to parrot back memorized information from a text or lecture, other questions strive to extend student learning beyond the concepts explicitly taught. Research shows that questions that involve higher-order thinking skills are more effective at enhancing student learning and advancing achievement than those that involve the simple recitation of learned material (Ibe 2009).

What makes an effective question? According to Fusco (2012), effective questions "build students' thinking by encouraging students to reflect on their ideas and compare their perceptions with those of others." In their book *Essential Questions*, McTighe and Wiggins (2013) explain that effective questions are generally open-ended, thought-provoking, and intellectually engaging. These questions necessitate higher-order thinking and address "important, transferable ideas within (and sometimes across) disciplines" (3). Essential questions lead to further inquiry, necessitate support and justification, and recur over time. These types of questions address foundational concepts that are essential for comprehension of a particular topic and they challenge students to think beyond the boundaries of their immediate knowledge to explore broader concepts. Regardless of the subject matter or content area, effective questions should be designed and used in the classroom to enhance learning, engage students' critical-thinking skills, and increase comprehension.

> Effective questions "build students' thinking by encouraging students to reflect on their ideas and compare their perceptions with those of others."
>
> (Fusco 2012)

The Importance of Text-Dependent Questions (cont.)

What Is a Text-Dependent Question?

A large portion of classroom learning involves the comprehension and analysis of text. Texts vary in content and style, from literary novels and dramas, to textbooks, newspaper articles, statistical reports, and Internet websites. Regardless of the format, students must be able to decode and comprehend the contents of the text in order to learn from the material. Research indicates that questions posed by teachers are essential for developing readers' abilities to successfully comprehend text (Kim 2010) and text-dependent questions are effective questions designed to achieve this goal. These types of questions increase students' understanding of the text through an in-depth examination of a particular aspect of a text. They guide students to examine a portion of the text and then provide evidence for their answers. Text-dependent questions help students explore the material presented explicitly in the text and also draw inferences based on that material. Unlike other types of questions, text-dependent questions rely solely on the text. Students do not necessarily need to access significant background knowledge or include outside information when answering a text-dependent question.

Text-dependent questions facilitate the comprehension of text on a variety of levels. On the most specific level, these questions help students analyze words and sentences within the text in order to determine the specific meaning and connotations of particular words and phrases. Text-dependent questions also enable students to study broader concepts, such as text structure and point of view. They aid students in their study of the individuals, settings, and sequences of events in a text and also provide a means for investigating the presence of other types of media within the writing (e.g., drawings, illustrations, graphs, tables). These questions also offer an effective tool for helping students analyze the overarching themes, concepts, arguments, and claims presented in texts. Finally, text-dependent questions help students build their abilities to compare multiple texts to each other on a variety of topics. Through thoughtful design and sequencing, text-dependent questions can be tailored to meet many specific educational standards and learning objectives while still maintaining a direct connection to the text.

With the advent of new standards in many states, such as the Common Core, one area of emphasis is close reading. Close reading involves "an investigation of a short piece of text, with multiple readings done over multiple instructional lessons. Through text-based questions and discussion, students are guided to deeply analyze and appreciate various aspects of the text" (Brown and Kappes 2012, 2). The practice of close reading has its roots in the first and last anchor standards for reading in the Common Core State Standards. The first anchor standard states that students should be able to "read closely to determine what the text says explicitly and to make logical inferences from it; cite specific textual evidence when writing or speaking to support conclusions drawn from the text" (National Governors Association Center 2010). In addition, anchor standard 10 mandates that students "read and comprehend complex literary and informational texts independently and proficiently" (National Governors Association Center 2010). Together, these two foundational standards require students

The Importance of Text-Dependent Questions *(cont.)*

to be able to perform in-depth, evidence-based analyses on complex texts, and the close reading strategy can help students achieve this goal.

The exact steps involved in close reading may vary from teacher to teacher, but the strategy always shares several of the same attributes. First, a teacher must select an appropriate text. Text selections for close reading should be complex enough to challenge students, yet not be completely beyond their reading level. The text should contain important ideas worthy of exploration and grade-appropriate vocabulary, syntax, and text structure. In general, a close reading text selection should be relatively brief to allow for multiple readings. Once an appropriate text is selected, students read the text, usually both independently and as a group. Next, students explore the text through text-based questions and small-group discussions that focus on distinct elements of the text. For example, the teacher may choose to have students study the usage of specific words or phrases, the presence of visual elements in the text, or the development of theme within the specific text passage. Finally, students synthesize the information gathered in either a whole-class discussion or writing activity (Nelson-Royes 2013, 43).

Text-dependent questions serve as the foundation for the close reading strategy. These questions help set the purpose for the close reading and guide students to carefully read and reread specific sections of the text in order to strengthen their understanding. Text-dependent questions also allow students to access complex texts that might be overwhelmingly challenging without the structure provided by the questions. Through a carefully structured progression of text-dependent questions, students learn how to deepen their comprehension of the text by asking and answering increasingly complex questions. Additionally, text-dependent questions help students learn to cite textual evidence to support their ideas. By continually directing students back to the text in search of evidence to support their conclusions, text-dependent questions show students the importance of validating their claims. For students with limited background knowledge or lower reading skills, the ability to use the close reading strategy to accurately comprehend complex texts offers an opportunity to accelerate their learning and increase their reading proficiency (Brown and Kappes 2012, 2). Ultimately, the goal is for students to be able to read and comprehend the subtleties and nuances of complex texts independently. Text-dependent questions provide the scaffolding and structure necessary for students to learn and eventually internalize the text by reading closely. Through text-dependent questions, students develop the necessary skills required to perform a close reading of a text by themselves.

> Text-dependent questions serve as the foundation for the close reading strategy.

The Importance of Text-Dependent Questions (cont.)

How are Text-Dependent Questions Used?

Text-dependent questions can be used to increase students' competency with reading comprehension in a variety of ways. In order to become proficient readers, students must develop a variety of different skills that fall under the term "reading comprehension." These skills include developing an understanding of inference, theme, supporting details, language usage, text structure, point of view, and other key text elements. The versatility of text-dependent questions allows teachers to craft questions to meet the specific demands of each individual skill.

Inference

By definition, inferences are not explicitly stated in the text; rather the reader must infer the implicit connection between pieces of information in order to understand the text. Oftentimes, students do not even realize when they have misunderstood or completely missed an inference in the text. They simply keep reading without ever gaining a full understanding of what is implied. This missed opportunity often affects their overall comprehension of the text. Text-dependent questions can call students' attention to the specific portion of the text containing the inference and highlight the structure of the language that makes the inference possible and necessary. In this way, text-dependent questions help students notice the fact that an inference is necessary, explicitly explain it, and examine the purpose behind the author's use of inference in the text. As students become more proficient with inferencing, text-dependent questions can move away from directing students to a specific opportunity for inferencing and allow them to select their own text-based evidence for support.

Central Ideas and Key Details

Text-dependent questions can also be used to help students identify overarching themes, key central ideas, and important supporting details. Depending on the text, the main themes or central ideas may be communicated implicitly or explicitly. While informational texts often present their central ideas in an explicit, straightforward manner, works of literature tend to develop their themes implicitly over the course of the text. Regardless of the presentation of these ideas, text-dependent questions enable readers to pull the important information from the larger body of writing and determine the central focus of the text. Furthermore, text-dependent questions help the reader revisit the text to identify the key details that support these central points. The identification and analysis of central ideas and key details allows the reader to internalize the most important information from the text while also gaining an understanding of the underlying supporting details.

The Importance of Text-Dependent Questions *(cont.)*

Individuals, Events, and Ideas

Text-dependent questions can serve as useful tools for exploring more explicit text elements, such as individuals, events, and ideas. From a young age, students are generally taught to identify the characters, setting, and plot sequences in stories. While this is important, questions that simply ask students to name these elements do not enhance their learning. Effective text-dependent questions challenge the reader to go beyond these basic facts and think about the why and how behind individuals, events, and ideas in a text. These questions push students to consider the author's purpose in creating or describing individuals in a particular way. They challenge students to look at the connections between characters, events, and ideas. For example, a text-dependent question might ask students to explore how plot sequence affects character development or how the setting affects the tone of the text. With a deeper understanding of how these fundamental text elements interact, students improve their comprehension of the intricacies behind complex texts and gain a greater understanding of the overall meaning of the text.

Language Usage

Text-dependent questions teach students to think about and analyze the way authors use specific words and phrases. English is complex, and words often have multiple meanings or connotations that can change depending on context. While skilled readers often surmise a word's meaning from its context, struggling readers frequently have trouble with the ambiguity that accompanies words with multiple meanings. Text-dependent questions can be used to show students how to use the context surrounding the word to determine its precise meaning in the text. In addition, text-dependent questions can help students study the use of figurative language and examine the ways in which specific words or phrases create tone, convey emotion, and enhance imagery in texts.

Text Structure

A thorough understanding of text structure is another vital component of reading comprehension. Text structure includes the sequence and order of information presented, the way the text is organized, the story structure, the relationship between units, the use of text features (table of contents, headings, italics, etc.), and much more. By understanding the underlying text structure of a piece of writing, students are better equipped to learn from the text in an efficient and organized manner. For literature, text-dependent questions help students examine story structure, including plot elements such as the introduction, conflict, and resolution. Students also learn to explore how the type of literature (story, poem, drama, etc.) plays a role in the structure of the text. Informational texts have different structures such as cause and effect or problem-solution, and often include many explicit text features, such as titles, headings, and captions, which are designed to help the reader access the text. Despite the explicit nature of these features, students often gloss over them or skip

The Importance of Text-Dependent Questions (cont.)

them altogether. By guiding their attention to the structure of the text, text-dependent questions teach students how to use and learn from these structures and features, ultimately improving their reading comprehension.

Point of View and Author's Purpose

The ability to identify and evaluate an author's purpose and point of view is a challenging skill that is related to reading comprehension. Every author writes his or her text with a purpose in mind. For example, the purpose of a text might be to educate, entertain, or persuade the reader. The author shapes the text to meet this purpose through word choice, style, tone, structure, content, and more. Furthermore, an author's point of view also plays a role in the development of a text. Authors express their points of view though literary techniques such as narration style, character development, and dialogue. While the purpose and point of view of a text may not be readily obvious to the reader during an initial reading of the text, these components clearly have a large impact on the overall effect of the text. Through the use of text-dependent questions, students can learn to recognize the author's purpose and point of view and delineate the ways in which these factors influence the text.

Arguments and Claims

One common purpose of informational writing is the presentation of an argument or claim about a given topic. Although students often learn to identify this type of writing and describe the argument or claim being presented, they generally fail to take their comprehension to the next step of evaluating the text. In order to be adequately prepared for the challenges of college and future careers, it is vital that students have the skills to not only comprehend an argument in a text, but also to critique the claim and assess its validity. Text-dependent questions are an excellent instrument to help students develop these skills. Because text-dependent questions rely exclusively on the text, students learn to evaluate arguments based on the reasons and evidence presented. Through text-dependent questions, students acquire the skills to identify arguments and claims, assess the presence and quality of the reasons behind the argument, and evaluate the general validity of the claim.

Compare and Contrast Multiple Texts

The ability to compare and contrast is a higher-level critical-thinking skill used to analyze two or more texts. Texts may be compared on a wide variety of different topics, including content, style, theme, and purpose. In order to compare multiple texts, students must first be able to identify and analyze the given topic in each independently and then be able to integrate this knowledge to reveal the similarities and differences between the texts. Because this area of analysis is so broad, text-dependent questions serve as useful guides to narrow students' focus of study and ensure that they use evidence from the text to support their reasoning. Simply

The Importance of Text-Dependent Questions (cont.)

asking students to compare multiple texts would be a daunting task for anyone, let alone struggling readers, but text-dependent questions can scaffold the task in order to make it accessible for all students. For example, a series of text-dependent questions might first ask students to compare and contrast two characters from separate texts. Once they understand how these two characters relate, the questions would guide them to further investigate the different techniques the authors use to develop these characters over the course of the texts. A final question would ask students to analyze how these different character-development techniques play a role in the formation of similar or distinct themes in the texts. By breaking down the formidable task of comparing and contrasting multiple texts, these questions enable students to understand the process used for in-depth analysis while also increasing their comprehension of multiple texts.

By using text-dependent questions to build reading comprehension, students learn the necessary skills to distinguish important elements of the text, analyze the ways in which these elements affect the style and content, and justify their thinking using evidence and information drawn directly from the text. Text-dependent questions not only strengthen students' understanding while reading in the classroom, but they also provide students with the scaffolding and structure necessary to internalize comprehension for reading independently outside of the classroom.

Writing

In addition to helping to build these reading comprehension skills, text-dependent questions also benefit students' writing skills. Research shows that what children read affects their writing and that reading activities can be used to improve writing skills (Maria 1990, 210). Text-dependent questions help students understand how authors create themes, communicate ideas, develop text structure, express emotions, and much more through written text. As students increase their awareness of these techniques through reading, they gain knowledge and strategies that they can apply to their own writing.

Text-dependent questions require students to refer back to the text in order to cite evidence to support their answers. As a result, text-dependent questions teach students how to create convincing arguments in their writing and justify their opinions with textual evidence. Depending on the format of the question, students may be required to summarize, paraphrase, or quote directly from the text. As students advance in their writing abilities, they learn how to accurately cite text, avoid plagiarism, and correctly reference an author's thoughts and ideas.

Overall, text-dependent questions serve as an instrumental tool in teaching students about many important concepts related to text. These questions not only facilitate students' abilities to understand a variety of texts on a deeper level, but they also provide practice with techniques and strategies that students can use to improve their own writing skills.

> Text-dependent questions serve as an instrumental tool in teaching students about many important concepts related to text.

The Importance of Text-Dependent Questions *(cont.)*

When Do You Use Text-Dependent Questions?

Text-dependent questions can be used any time students need to read and comprehend a piece of text. These questions are designed to help students focus on certain aspects of the text in order to learn skills and content from the reading. They can be incorporated into multiple lessons about the same selection of text or be used with different selections focusing on the same concept. In a language arts lesson for example, a teacher may choose to use text-dependent questions over the course of a unit on Shakespeare's *Romeo and Juliet* to help students analyze the text for character development, figurative language, point of view, etc. Alternatively, a teacher may use the same set of text-dependent questions over several days to examine a single concept, such as theme, using a variety of text selections from different sources.

Text-dependent questions are very adaptable and can be used in almost any situation that involves text analysis. That being said, these questions often serve students best when posed after at least one, and sometimes more, readings of the text. When doing a close reading of a text, for example, many teachers choose to have students read the text independently for the first reading, and then as a group for the second reading. The initial reading gives students the chance to experience the text and form their own ideas, while the second reading allows them to experience the language of the text by listening to others read it aloud. Then, during the third reading, the teacher introduces the text-dependent questions and students engage in a discussion, citing evidence from the text to support their points and reading selections of the text aloud when appropriate. These discussions are generally followed by a writing exercise and other text-related activities (McLaughlin and Overturf 2013, 225). By using text-dependent questions for the foundation of the text analysis, the teacher ensures that the discussion remains focused on the text and that students consistently validate their thoughts and opinions with textual evidence. Text-dependent questions may also be used as part of the activities that follow the discussion to guide writing assignments or focus further study.

Where Do You Use Text-Dependent Questions?

Text-dependent questions can be used to facilitate the comprehension and understanding of any type of text. These strategies can, and should, be applied to any type of text across disciplines and content areas. For example, text-dependent questions can be used in the science classroom to facilitate the understanding of the research behind a scientific argument. Text-based artifacts, such as letters and speeches, provide excellent opportunities for the use of text-dependent questions in the social studies classroom. Biographies and autobiographies of leaders in any discipline offer ample opportunity for in-depth study through text-dependent questions as well.

The Importance of Text-Dependent Questions *(cont.)*

Text-dependent questions may be used with both literature and informational texts. As you will see throughout this resource, some question stems can be used with either type of text while others are designed specifically to address either literature or informational text. In some situations, especially with younger students, these questions should be used with very brief text passages. Students in the lower grades will benefit from passages that are only a few sentences long. Students with greater reading skills can apply text-dependent questions to longer text passages, but the selections should still be short enough to allow for multiple readings.

In addition to their role in text-based discussions involving the whole class, text-dependent questions can be used for a variety of other purposes. Students can use these questions to guide text analyses on homework assignments and teachers can use them to gauge comprehension on assessments. They can also be used to facilitate discussions among small groups or pairs of students. Since text-dependent questions require students to provide evidence from the text to support their answers, these questions have the beneficial effect of making it harder for students to get off-topic during small-group discussions. Other types of questions that ask students to refer to their background knowledge or prior experiences leave more room for deviation from the text and the questions at hand.

How Do You Create Text-Dependent Questions?

This book offers a wide range of text-dependent questions that can be used to increase reading comprehension in a number of different areas. However, each text, lesson plan, and curriculum is different and it may be necessary to create other text-dependent questions to supplement or support the ones supplied in this book.

When considering what type of text-dependent questions to ask, it is important to think about the key ideas in the text and the desired outcomes of the lesson. What should students understand at the end of the lesson? What are the core concepts that this text teaches? Once these main ideas and objectives have been identified, then the teacher should determine the particular aspects of the text that should be studied in order for students to reach this understanding. The teacher should examine key vocabulary words and important text structures that are related to the underlying core concepts and develop questions that highlight these connections. Furthermore, the teacher should identify complex sections of the text that may prove difficult for students and create questions that allow students to address and master the challenges presented by the text.

When developing text-dependent questions, teachers may also choose to start with the national or state standards that serve as the basis for their lesson plans. By looking at the key nouns and verbs, teachers can craft questions that highlight the important concepts in each standard (McTighe and Wiggins 2013, 29). For example, a third grade teacher might start by picking a Common Core English Language Arts standard, such as anchor standard 3 which reads, "Analyze how and why individuals,

The Importance of Text-Dependent Questions *(cont.)*

events, or ideas develop and interact over the course of a text" (National Governors Association Center 2010). For third grade, the literature standard in this strand is "Describe characters in a story (e.g., their traits, motivations, or feelings) and explain how their actions contribute to the sequence of events." In this example, the key nouns and verbs are *describe, characters, actions,* and *sequence of events.* The standard requires students to study the connections between the characters, their actions, and the story's sequence of events. Using this standard, the teacher can use this resource to craft text-dependent questions that guide students to examine various aspects of the character in the story. Once students gain an in-depth understanding of the characters, the teacher can introduce additional text-dependent questions that lead students to analyze the relationship between the sequence of events in the text and the characters' actions.

It is also important to consider the sequence of the text-dependent questions presented to students. Generally, the opening questions should be more straightforward, giving students an opportunity to become familiar with the text and removing any technical obstacles, such as challenging vocabulary words, which could hinder comprehension. After students gain a basic understanding of the text, the teacher can introduce more complex questions that strive to illuminate the broader, more intricate concepts. By scaffolding the questions to move from basic, concrete topics to elaborate, implied concepts, teachers can use text-dependent questions to guide students to a detailed understanding of the complexities of a text.

How Do You Set the Stage for Text Analysis in the Classroom?

> Text-dependent questions are designed to stimulate critical-thinking skills and increase reading comprehension.

When using questioning strategies for text analysis, it is vital to establish a safe and collaborative classroom environment. Text-dependent questions are designed to stimulate critical-thinking skills and increase reading comprehension. It is building these skills, not getting the "right answer," that is the ultimate goal, and students may need to be reminded of this fact. Indeed, many text-dependent questions are open-ended and do not have a single, correct answer. In order to ensure a collaborative classroom environment, students need to be confident that their answers to questions and their contributions to classroom discussions will be respected by everyone in the room. Before delving into a discussion, review a set of clear guidelines that outlines appropriate responses and reactions during discussions. In addition to these guidelines, it is important to provide students with constructive ways to express their disagreement or challenge another student's assumptions or analysis of a text. For instance, teach students how to ask probing questions, such as "How do you know _____?" or "What's your reasoning?" (McTighe and Wiggins 2013, 56). These types of questions will advance the discussion and encourage students to refer back to the text for evidence to further support their responses.

The Importance of Text-Dependent Questions (cont.)

Ideally, the teacher should play the role of facilitator, rather than instructor, during a classroom discussion using text-dependent questions. By supplying the class with an open-ended question that reflects a central idea or theme, the teacher provides a launching point for students to collaboratively investigate various aspects of the text. Throughout the discussion, the teacher may provide additional questions that enable students to focus on particular areas or concepts within the text. Then, with their newfound insights, the teacher can guide students to bring this information together in order to revisit the initial central question at the end of the discussion. Initially, the teacher may need to direct students back to the text if the discussion starts to move away from the area of focus, but through the continued use of text-dependent questions, students will eventually learn to redirect themselves by requesting and providing textual evidence to support their ideas.

In conclusion, text-dependent questions are an important and versatile tool for building reading comprehension and higher-level thinking skills. The Common Core and other state standards require that students be able to analyze complex texts, while also providing textual evidence to support their ideas. Text-dependent questions are the ideal instruments for helping students achieve these goals. Text-dependent questions show students how to break down difficult sections of text, clarify challenging vocabulary words, examine text structure, investigate inferences, scrutinize claims, and much more. These questions teach students how to accurately cite text and serve as the basis for engaging discussions about significant questions. In the ever-changing realm of our education system, text-dependent questions offer teachers and students an effective approach to improving reading comprehension across grade levels and content areas.

How to Use This Book

TDQs Strategies for Building Text-Dependent Questions is a versatile resource that can be used to support the implementation of text-dependent questions in the K–12 classroom. This resource provides teachers with an overview of each section, sample text-dependent questions/prompts, and sample literary and informational text passages for grades K–12, along with corresponding questions/prompts. The sample text passages are meant to serve as models for the teacher and can be modified as desired to meet the needs of students.

- **Overview**—This section tells the reader what to expect and provides background knowledge about the topic.

- **Text-Dependent Questions/Prompts**—This section provides sample text-dependent questions/prompts that can be used in a classroom with students to support any type of book.

- **Literary and Informational Text Passages**—This section provides sample text passages for grade spans K–1, 2–3, 4–5, 6–8, and 9–12. Each passage also includes corresponding text-dependent questions/prompts. Depending on the reading level of your students, you may choose to read the passages aloud, have students read in pairs or small groups, or instruct students to read independently.

- **Digital Resource CD**—The CD contains digital versions of the model text passages and questions/prompts.

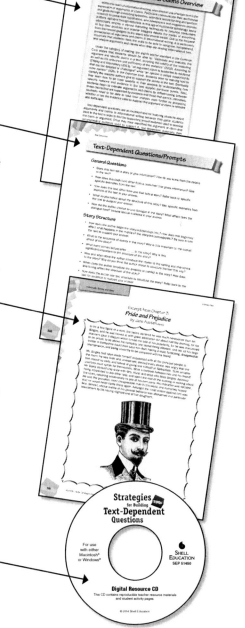

Inference

Text-dependent questions (TDQs) are important to the understanding of inference. In this section, you will find an overview, sample text-dependent questions/prompts, literary and informational passages, as well as supporting questions/prompts to use with your students. Below is a chart that provides the titles and the recommended grade ranges for the texts in this section.

Grade Range	Literary Text	Page #	Informational Text	Page #
K–1	*The Storm*	24	*The Brain*	26
2–3	*Why the Woodpecker Bores for Its Food*	28	*Our Earth*	32
4–5	Excerpt from *The Wind in the Willows* by Kenneth Grahame	35	*The World of Animals*	38
6–8	Excerpt from *The Rover Boys at School* by Edward Stratemeyer	41	*James Madison: Architect of the Constitution*	44
9–12	Excerpt from Chapter 1, *King Arthur and His Knights* by Sir James Knowles	46	Excerpt from *Origin and Development of Form and Ornament in Ceramic Art* by William H. Holmes	50

Inference Overview

Teaching the skill of inference often provides a significant challenge for teachers. An inference occurs when a reader draws a conclusion about something that is not explicitly stated in the text. In order to make inferences while reading, readers must go beyond the literal meaning of the words on the page. According to Bintz et al., readers must be "active" and "curious" so they can "use background knowledge, and recognize text clues to make sense of text" (2012, 17). Consider the following text: "Sam whispered something into Andy's ear. Andy ran off crying." The reader will likely make the inference that whatever Sam whispered to Andy caused him to get upset. This inference is based on the knowledge that people cry when they are hurt or upset and that whispering is often used to communicate something that one does not want other people to overhear, such as mean or hurtful statements. In order to make this inference from the text, the reader must ask him or herself, "Why did Andy start crying?" and extract evidence from the text to infer an answer.

There are several different main types of inferences that occur while reading a text (Kispal 2008). These types include: coherence, elaborative, and global inferences. **Coherence inferences** happen when the reader must infer something from other information in the text. For example, in the sentences "Jon ran back to get his helmet. He put it on and jumped on his bike," the reader must infer that the pronoun "he" refers to Jon and the pronoun "it" refers to his helmet. **Elaborative inferences** require the reader to use prior knowledge to supply the connection between the ideas or sentences in the text. The example with Andy in the previous paragraph is an elaborative inference. Finally, **global inferences** deal with the comprehension of overarching themes or ideas in the text. This section primarily focuses on coherence and elaborative inferences while the next section covers global inferences alongside theme.

The first reading anchor standard in the Common Core State Standards (2010) highlights the importance of inference. It states that students should be able to "read closely to determine what the text says explicitly and to make logical inferences from it." Through the use of text-dependent questions, students learn to examine the text and differentiate between ideas and concepts that are stated explicitly versus implicitly. Once they are able to make this distinction, students can analyze the inferences made from the text to see the ways in which they contribute to the overall text. In other words, text-dependent questions "allow students to consider the information that is provided and then make informed extrapolations from the information provided" (Fisher and Frey 2012, 6). In addition, text-dependent questions help students validate their inferences through the text. Occasionally, students erroneously base their inferences entirely on background knowledge without connecting them to text, leading to faulty inferences that can interfere with comprehension. Text-dependent questions require the student to link his or her inference to the text, thereby ensuring a relevant connection.

Text-Dependent Questions/Prompts

General Inference Questions

- Reread the sentence that starts with "_____." What does the sentence say explicitly? What can you infer from it?

- What inference does the author want you to make from the _____ sentence/paragraph? Support your answer with evidence from the text.

- What word/phrase did the author use to describe _____? What does this word choice make you infer?

- What do you infer from the _____ paragraph? What does it say explicitly?

- Reread the _____ paragraph. List the facts that are explicitly stated in the text. Write at least one inference that you made while reading the paragraph.

Coherence Inference Questions

- How does inference connect the following two sentences: "_____" and "_____"?

- In the _____ sentence/paragraph, the author uses the word "_____." What does the word "_____" refer to? How do you know?

- How does the author use inference to connect the individual sentences in the _____ paragraph? Include specific examples from the text to support your answer.

- How does the use of pronouns in the _____ sentence affect the flow of the paragraph? Cite examples from the text to support your opinion.

- In the sentence, "_____" what does the word "_____" refer to? Why is it important to know this in order to understand the sentence?

- What can you infer from the text structure? How is your inference supported by evidence from the text?

- How does the author's use of _____ in the text structure affect what you infer from the text? Support your answer with evidence from the text.

- What is the reader expected to infer from the figurative language in the _____ paragraph? Justify your answer with specific examples from the text.

Elaborative Inference Questions

- In the _____ paragraph, the author says, "_____." What does this mean? What general knowledge did you use to make this inference?

- Why did _____ feel _____ in paragraph/sentence _____? How do you know? Include specific words and phrases from the text in your answer.

- What does the author tell you explicitly in the _____ paragraph? What background knowledge did you use to make an inference about this information?

Text-Dependent Questions/Prompts (cont.)

- Reread the _____ sentence/paragraph. What general knowledge allowed you to connect this information with the rest of the text? Refer back to the text for specific examples.

- What can you infer about _____ by the end of the _____ paragraph? How do you know?

- Reread the _____ sentence/paragraph. What do you know explicitly from this sentence? What personal knowledge do you incorporate to make an inference about _____?

- What do you infer from the characters' actions in the _____ paragraph? How do you know?

- What inferences can you make from the dialogue in the _____ paragraph? What evidence from the text supports these inferences?

- What emotions do the characters experience in the _____ sentence/paragraph? How did you infer what they were feeling without the author stating it explicitly? Reference specific examples from the text to support your answer.

- What is the main point of the _____ paragraph? Did the author communicate it implicitly or explicitly? Explain your answer using examples from the text.

- What does the author already expect you to know about _____ in the _____ paragraph/sentence to understand the text? How do you know? Refer to specific examples from the text to justify your answer.

- How does the narrator feel in the passage? How do you know? Include textual evidence to support your answer.

- Reread the _____ paragraph/sentence. What does the author explicitly tell you about the setting? What can you infer? Support your answer with textual evidence.

- What can you infer about the characters' personalities from their actions? What part of the text supports your inference(s)?

- How does the _____ sentence help you activate your personal knowledge about the topic? Why is this important in the text?

- What is the purpose of the sentence "_____"? How does this sentence help you make inferences about _____?

- What can you infer from the character's action in this sentence: "_____"? What evidence in the text supports this inference?

- Reread the _____ paragraph. What can you infer about _____ relationship with _____ from this paragraph?

The Storm

The sky was dark. It was very windy. A door banged shut outside.

My window rattled. I tried to sleep, but I couldn't.

Suddenly, my nightlight went out. I flipped the switch, but it wouldn't come back on.

My room was completely black. I hid my head under the covers and waited for my parents to come get me.

Name: _____ Date: _____

The Storm (cont.)

Directions: Use the text to answer the questions below.

1 In the third paragraph, the author uses the word "it." What does the word "it" refer to? How do you know?

_____

_ _ _ _ _ _ _ _ _ _ _ _ _ _ _ _ _ _ _

_____
_____

_ _ _ _ _ _ _ _ _ _ _ _ _ _ _ _ _ _ _

_____
_____

_ _ _ _ _ _ _ _ _ _ _ _ _ _ _ _ _ _ _

_____

2 How does the narrator feel in the passage? How do you know?

_____

_ _ _ _ _ _ _ _ _ _ _ _ _ _ _ _ _ _ _

_____
_____

_ _ _ _ _ _ _ _ _ _ _ _ _ _ _ _ _ _ _

_____
_____

_ _ _ _ _ _ _ _ _ _ _ _ _ _ _ _ _ _ _

_____

The Brain

Your brain is a soft organ. It is inside your head. The bone around your brain is called your skull. Your skull protects your brain.

Your brain controls your body. It stores information in your memory. This is how you learn. It also tells your muscles when to move. It moves your legs when you run. It even tells your eye muscles when to blink!

Your feelings also come from your brain. How do you feel when you cut your finger? Your brain sends out a signal that makes you feel the pain from the cut. It also controls your mood. It makes you feel happy, sad, or scared. Your brain is very important!

Name: _____ Date: _____

The Brain (cont.)

Directions: Use the text to answer the questions below.

1 Reread the fourth sentence. What inference can you make about how the skull protects the brain?

_____

-- -- -- -- -- -- -- -- -- -- -- -- --

_____

_____

-- -- -- -- -- -- -- -- -- -- -- -- --

_____

_____

-- -- -- -- -- -- -- -- -- -- -- -- --

_____

2 What is the purpose of the sentence "How do you feel when you cut your finger?" How does this sentence help you make inferences about the text?

_____

-- -- -- -- -- -- -- -- -- -- -- -- --

_____

_____

-- -- -- -- -- -- -- -- -- -- -- -- --

_____

_____

-- -- -- -- -- -- -- -- -- -- -- -- --

_____

Why the Woodpecker Bores for Its Food
Excerpt from *Stories the Iroquois Tell Their Children*
by Mabel Powers

Once upon a time, the Great Spirit left the Happy Hunting Ground and came to Earth. He took the form of a poor, hungry man. He went from wigwam to wigwam, asking for food.

One day, he came to a wigwam in which a woman was baking cakes. "I am very hungry," the man said. "Will you please give me a cake?"

The woman looked at the man, and then at the cake. She saw that it was too large to give away. She said, "I will not give you this cake, but I will bake you one, if you will wait." The hungry man said, "I will wait."

Then the woman took a small piece of dough and made it into a cake and baked it. But when she took this cake from the coals, it was larger than the first. Again the woman looked at her cake. Again she saw it was too large to give away. Again she said, "I will not give you this one, but I will bake you one, if you will wait." Again the man said, "I will wait."

This time the woman took a very, very, tiny bit of dough, and made it into a cake. "Surely, this will be small enough to give away," she thought, yet when baked it was larger than both the others. The woman looked at the three cakes. Each was too large to give away.

Why the Woodpecker Bores for Its Food
Excerpt from *Stories the Iroquois Tell Their Children*
by Mabel Powers *(cont.)*

"I will not give you any of the cakes," she said to the man. "Go to the woods, and find your food in the bark of trees."

Then the man stood up and threw off his ragged blanket and worn moccasins. His face shone like the sun, and he was very beautiful. The woman shrank into the shadow of the wigwam.

"I am the Great Spirit," said he, "and you are a selfish woman. People should be kind, and generous, and unselfish. You shall no longer be a person and live in a warm wigwam, with plenty of cakes to bake. You shall go to the forest and hunt your food in the bark of trees. You shall eat worms of the same size as the cake you would have made for me."

The woman began to grow smaller and smaller. Feathers grew upon her body and wings sprang from it. The Great Spirit touched her head, and it became red.

"Always shall you wear this red hood," he said, "as a mark of your shame. Always shall you hide from man. Always shall you hunt for little worms, the size of the cake you made for me."

At this a sharp cry was heard, and a bird flew into the fireplace of the wigwam, and up the chimney. As it passed out of the chimney, the soot left those long streaks of black which we see now on the woodpecker's back. Ever since then, this woodpecker has had a red head, and has been hiding from man on the farther side of the tree trunk while boring in the bark for little worms.

Name: _____ Date: _____

Why the Woodpecker Bores for Its Food
Excerpt from *Stories the Iroquois Tell Their Children*
by Mabel Powers *(cont.)*

Directions: Use the text to answer the questions below.

1 How does your personal background knowledge help you understand why the woman refuses to give the Great Spirit the large cakes? How does the text support this understanding? Refer explicitly to the text in your answer.

_____

_____

_____

_____

2 What can you infer from the character's action in the sentence that says, "The woman shrank into the shadow of the wigwam"? What evidence in the text supports this inference?

_____

_____

_____

_____

Name: _____ Date: _____

Why the Woodpecker Bores for Its Food
Excerpt from *Stories the Iroquois Tell Their Children*
by **Mabel Powers** *(cont.)*

3 How does the author's use of repetition in the text structure affect what you infer from the text? Support your answer with evidence from the text.

_____

_____

_____

_____

Our Earth

Earth is an interesting place. There's a lot to see and do. There's a lot to figure out, too. Earth can tell us about itself. How? That's simple. Just take a look around. Try digging. Go exploring. Earth reveals much about its past.

Fossils are evidence of past life. They are the remains or imprints of living things from long ago. They can be leaf prints or footprints. They can also be shell prints or skeleton prints. The waste from livings things can even become fossils!

Fossils are made in different ways. They can be made when a living thing dies. The living thing becomes buried by **sediments**. Sediments are things such as mud and sand. Ash from a volcano and **silt** are also sediments. Fossils can also be frozen in ice. Some fossils have even been buried in tar for thousands of years.

Most fossils are made when the soft parts of a living thing decay. The hard parts are turned into something like rock. The minerals in the sediments seep into the hard parts of the living thing. They become preserved as fossils. Other fossils are made when the whole living thing is frozen or mummified. Then, the soft parts are included, too.

Our Earth (cont.)

Fossils are more likely to be made when a living thing dies near water than on dry land. Near water, it is likely to be quickly buried. Over thousands of years, the sediments settle into layers that become **sedimentary** rock. Fossils are often found in this type of rock.

Scientists have been studying Earth for a long time. Some of the first geologists came from ancient Greece and Egypt. They learned some of the basics of **geology**. They discovered that fossils were the remains of animals and plants. Fossils tell the story of Earth's past and help us understand what it may have been like many years ago. Without fossils, we may have never made the important discoveries that have helped scientists make predictions about Earth's future, too!

Name: _____ Date: _____

Our Earth (cont.)

Directions: Use the text to answer the questions below.

1 How does the author use inference to connect the individual sentences in the first paragraph? Include specific examples from the text to support your answer.

_____

_____

_____

2 In the fourth paragraph, the author says, "The hard parts are turned into something like rock." What does this mean? What general knowledge did you use to make this inference? Support your knowledge with examples from the text.

_____

_____

_____

3 Describe an inference you made when reading the last paragraph. What combination of prior knowledge and textual evidence allowed you to make this inference?

_____

_____

_____

Excerpt from
The Wind in the Willows
by Kenneth Grahame

"But what I wanted to ask you was, won't you take me to call on Mr. Toad? I've heard so much about him, and I do so want to make his acquaintance."

"Why certainly," said the good-natured Rat, jumping to his feet and dismissing poetry from his mind for the day. "Get the boat out, and we'll paddle up there at once. It's never the wrong time to call on Toad. Always good-tempered, always glad to see you, always sorry when you go!"

"He must be a very nice animal," observed the Mole, as he got into the boat next to Rat.

"He is indeed the best of animals," replied Rat. "So simple, so good-natured, and so affectionate. Perhaps he's not very clever—we can't all be geniuses; and it may be that he is both boastful and conceited. But he has got some great qualities, has Toady."

Rounding a bend in the river, they came in sight of a handsome, dignified old house of mellowed red brick, with well-kept lawns reaching down to the water's edge.

"There's Toad Hall," said the Rat, "and that creek on the left, where the notice-board says, 'Private. No landing allowed!' leads to his boathouse, where we'll leave the boat. The stables are over to the right. Toad is rather rich, you know, and this is really one of the nicest houses in these parts, though we never admit as much to Toad."

They disembarked, and strolled across the flower-decked lawns in search of Toad, whom they presently happened upon resting in a wicker garden chair, with a preoccupied expression on his face, and a large map spread out on his knees.

Excerpt from
The Wind in the Willows
by Kenneth Grahame *(cont.)*

"Hooray!" he cried, jumping up on seeing them, "This is splendid!" He shook the paws of both of them warmly, never waiting for an introduction to the Mole. "How KIND of you!" he went on, dancing round them. "I was just going to send a boat down the river for you, Ratty, with strict orders that you were to be fetched up here at once, whatever you were doing. I want you badly—both of you. Now what will you take? Come inside and have something! You don't know how lucky it is, your turning up just now!

"Let's sit quiet a bit, Toady!" said the Rat, throwing himself into an easy chair, while the Mole took another by the side of him and made some civil remark about Toad's delightful residence.

"Finest house on the whole river," cried Toad boisterously. "Or anywhere else, for that matter," he could not help adding.

Here the Rat nudged the Mole. Unfortunately the Toad saw him do it, and turned very red. There was a moment's painful silence. Then Toad burst out laughing. "All right, Ratty," he said. "It's only my way, you know. And it's not such a very bad house, is it? You know you rather like it yourself. Now, look here. Let's be sensible. You are the very animals I wanted. You've got to help me. It's most important!"

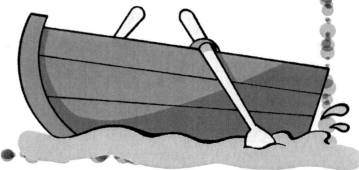

Name: _____   Date: _____

Excerpt from
The Wind in the Willows
by Kenneth Grahame (cont.)

Directions: Use the text to answer the questions below.

1 What inferences can you make from the dialogue in the first two paragraphs? What evidence from the text supports these inferences?

_____

_____

_____

2 What can you infer about Rat by the end of the third paragraph? How do you know?

_____

_____

_____

3 Reread the paragraph that starts with, "There's Toad Hall..." What can you infer about Rat's relationship with Toad from this paragraph?

_____

_____

_____

4 What emotions do the characters experience in the last paragraph? How did you infer what they were feeling without the author stating it explicitly? Be sure to reference specific examples from the text to support your answer.

_____

_____

_____

The World of Animals

What do you think of when you hear the word *animal*? You probably think of cats and dogs, or maybe cows or deer. Maybe you think of lizards or whales or even frogs. Do you think of bugs? What about fish? Does the word *animal* make you think of lobsters, sea slugs, or earthworms? These are all members of the animal kingdom.

Some animals we see every day. However, there are many more animals in the world that you might not see on a regular day. Some of them are very strange, like fish that can flip from one pond to another. There are octopuses that can open jars with their tentacles. There is the platypus, which has fur like a cat, a bill like a duck, and a tail like a beaver.

There is one animal, though, that you do see every day. It is the human being! You are a member of the animal kingdom, too. You are very different from fish, octopuses, and platypuses, but there are a lot of things that you have in common. First, living things are made of cells, and animals are made of more than one cell. Second, animal cells do not have cell walls like plant cells do. Third, all animals eat other organisms.

Scientists who study animals are called zoologists. Zoologists need to know exactly which animals other zoologists are talking about. They need to show how animals are alike and different. To do this, they use a system called *taxonomy*. Taxonomy is a system of classification. To classify things means to organize them into groups.

Imagine you worked at a car lot. You have many different cars. You have red cars, blue cars, and white cars. You have trucks, sedans, and convertibles. You have cars that run on gas and cars that use electricity. How could you organize them? You might divide them into two groups, cars and trucks, and then divide each group into four-doors and two-doors.

The World of Animals (cont.)

Zoologists use taxonomy in the same way. Taxonomy has six main groups called kingdoms. The kingdom *Animalia* is for animals. It is just one of the kingdoms. Plants, fungi, and microorganisms have their own kingdoms.

A zoologist can talk about an animal by using its scientific name. She might say, "*Felis silvestris* make good pets." Other zoologists know she is talking about house cats. Or she can talk about a whole group of animals and use the group's scientific name. She can say "*Felidae* eat meat." Other scientists know she is talking about all kinds of cats, such as tigers, panthers, and even house cats.

Taxonomy keeps dividing. It spreads out like a tree. Kingdoms are divided into groups called **phyla** and each phylum divides into smaller categories called **classes**. Classes are split into **orders** and orders have **families**. The next category is **genus**, and finally **species**. Every living thing goes into a category at each level.

The animal kingdom has many unique and special members. The next time you are outside, see how many you can count.

Name: _____   Date: _____

The World of Animals *(cont.)*

Directions: Use the text to answer the questions below.

1 In the sentence, "Zoologists use taxonomy in the same way," what do the words "same way" refer to? Why is it important to know this to understand the sentence?

_____

_____

_____

2 How does the author use inference to connect the individual sentences in the second paragraph? Include specific examples from the text to support your answer.

_____

_____

_____

3 What is the main point of the seventh paragraph? Did the author communicate it implicitly or explicitly? Explain your answer using examples from the text.

_____

_____

_____

4 What can you infer about zoologists by reading this text? How do you know?

_____

_____

_____

#51449—TDQs: Strategies for Building Text-Dependent Questions   © *Shell Education*

Excerpt from
The Rover Boys at School
by Edward Stratemeyer

They went into the station, procured tickets, and then found that the time for the train had been delayed. It would not be along for nearly half an hour or more.

"Good, just wait till I get back," said Tom.

He had noticed Ricks, the station master, gathering up some waste paper around the depot, and felt tolerably certain the old fellow was about to build a bonfire with it. Sauntering over to one of the stores, Tom entered and asked the proprietor if he had any large firecrackers on hand.

"Just two, sir," said the storekeeper, and brought them forth, showing that each was six inches long and thick in proportion.

"How much are they?" asked the boy.

"Seeing as they are the last I have, I'll let you have them for fifteen cents each."

"I'll give you a quarter for the two."

"Very well, here you are," and the transfer was made on the spot. Then, concealing the firecrackers into his coat pocket, Tom sauntered up to old Ricks while Sam and Dick looked on.

"Ricks, that is pretty bad news from Middletown, isn't it?" he observed.

"Bad news, what do you mean?" demanded the station master, as he threw some more waste paper on the fire that he had just lit.

"About that dynamite being stolen by the train wreckers. They think some of the explosive was brought up here."

"Didn't hear of it."

"Dynamite is pretty bad stuff to have around, so I've heard."

"Awful, awful, and I never want to see any of it," answered Ricks decidedly.

"If it goes off, it's apt to blow everything to splinters," said Dick.

"That's so, and I don't want any of it," said the old man as he began to gather up more waste paper for his fire. Watching for his chance, Tom threw one of the firecrackers into the blaze and then quickly rejoined his brothers.

Excerpt from
The Rover Boys at School
by Edward Stratemeyer *(cont.)*

With a handful of paper, Ricks again approached the blaze and was standing almost over the fire when the firecracker exploded.

"Help, I'm killed!" yelled old Ricks, as he fell upon his back. "Get me away from here, there's dynamite in this fire!" And he rolled over, leapt to his feet, and ran off like a madman.

"Don't be alarmed—it was only a firecracker," called out Tom, loud enough for all standing around to hear, and then he ran for the train that had just arrived. Soon he and his brothers were on board and off, leaving behind poor Ricks to be heartily laughed at by those who had observed the old man's sudden terror.

Name: _____ Date: _____

Excerpt from
The Rover Boys at School
by Edward Stratemeyer *(cont.)*

Directions: Use the text to answer the questions below.

1 What does the author already expect you to know about firecrackers in the third paragraph? How do you know? Refer to specific examples from the text to justify your answer.

_____

_____

_____

_____

2 What can you infer about the characters' personalities from their actions? What part of the text supports your inference(s)?

_____

_____

_____

_____

3 Reread the dialogue that starts with, "Ricks, that is pretty bad news from Middletown..." What can you infer about Tom's relationship with Ricks from this dialogue?

_____

_____

_____

_____

4 What emotions does Ricks experience in the passage? How did you infer what he was feeling without the author stating it explicitly? Reference specific examples from the text to support your answer.

_____

_____

_____

_____

James Madison: Architect of the Constitution

James Madison was born in Virginia in 1751. He grew up on his family's plantation. They had many slaves. Madison went to college in New Jersey. He studied the works of classic thinkers at this time.

Then Madison became involved in the American Revolution. In 1776, he went to the convention in Virginia. He voted whether or not to approve the Declaration of Independence. He also helped Virginia write its own state constitution.

Madison was elected to the Continental Congress in 1779. He wanted to create a stronger government. He thought that the Articles of Confederation was too weak to protect the country. Madison was a member of the Nationalist political group. This party wanted a strong central government.

Madison supported several parts of our government that still exist today. He wanted a supreme court. He also wanted a strong executive branch and a legislative branch with two groups. Madison worked hard to convince people to ratify the Constitution. He debated heavily with Patrick Henry at the Virginia ratification convention. Madison won. He convinced Virginia representatives to support the Constitution. Madison was elected to the new House of Representatives. He sponsored the Bill of Rights. The Bill of Rights was added to the Constitution later. He also worked closely with George Washington during this time.

After a few years, Madison began to disagree with his fellow party members. He started working with Thomas Jefferson. They both favored commerce with Britain and France. In 1801, Jefferson appointed Madison as secretary of state. Madison helped Jefferson negotiate the Louisiana Purchase. This became very important to the growth of the nation.

Madison was elected as the fourth president of the United States in 1808. He had a difficult time at first. He struggled to negotiate with Britain for commerce and trade. Madison declared war on Britain in 1812. He was still reelected, but the War of 1812 created a lot of problems during his presidency. In 1814, the British attacked Washington D.C. They burned it. The American soldiers eventually defeated the British. Things became easier for Madison. He ended his presidency with people pleased with his efforts to support the country. He died in 1836.

Name: _____   Date: _____

James Madison: Architect of the Constitution (cont.)

Directions: Use the text to answer the questions below.

1   What is the purpose of the sentence "He studied the works of classic thinkers at this time"? How does this sentence help you make inferences about James Madison?

_____

_____

_____

_____

2   How does the author use inference to connect the individual sentences in the fourth paragraph? Include specific examples from your text to support your answer.

_____

_____

_____

_____

3   Reread the paragraph that starts with, "Madison supported..." What can you infer about Madison's relationship with Patrick Henry from this paragraph?

_____

_____

_____

_____

4   Describe an inference you made when reading the last paragraph. What combination of prior knowledge and textual evidence allowed you to make this inference?

_____

_____

_____

_____

Excerpt from Chapter 1,
King Arthur and His Knights
by Sir James Knowles

King Vortigern the usurper sat upon his throne in London, when, suddenly, upon a certain day, in burst a breathless messenger who cried aloud—

"Arise, Lord King, for the enemy is come. Ambrosius and Uther, upon whose throne thou sittest, and a full twenty thousand men with them, have sworn by a great oath, Lord, to slay thee before this year be done. Even now they march towards thee as the north wind of winter for bitterness and haste."

At those words Vortigern's face grew white as ashes, and, rising in confusion and disorder, he sent for all the best artificers and craftsmen and mechanics, and commanded them vehemently to go and build him straightway in the furthest west of his lands a great and strong castle, where he might fly for refuge and escape the vengeance of his master's sons—"and, moreover," cried he, "let the work be done within a hundred days from now, or I will surely spare no life amongst you all."

Then all the host of craftsmen, fearing for their lives, found out a proper site whereon to build the tower, and eagerly began to lay in the foundations. But no sooner were the walls raised up above the ground than all their work was overwhelmed and broken down by night invisibly, no man perceiving how, or by whom, or what. And when the same thing happened again, and yet again, all the workmen, full of terror, sought out the king, and threw themselves upon their faces before him, beseeching him to interfere and help them or to deliver them from their dreadful work.

Filled with mixed rage and terror, the king called for the astrologers and wizards, and took counsel with them. He asked them what these things might be and how one might overcome them. The wizards worked their spells and incantations, and in the end declared that nothing but the blood of a youth born without mortal father, smeared on the foundations of the castle, could avail to make it stand. Messengers were therefore sent forth through all the land to find, if it were possible, such a child. And, as some of them went down a particular village street, they saw a band of belligerent lads fighting and quarrelling, and heard them bellow at one—"Flee, thou scallywag! Son of no mortal man! Go, find thy father, and leave us in peace."

At that the messengers looked steadfastly on the downtrodden lad, and asked who he was. The boys replied that his name was Merlin, that his birth and parentage were known by no man, and that the foul fiend alone was his father. Upon hearing the things, the officers seized Merlin, and carried him before the king by force.

Excerpt from Chapter 1,
King Arthur and His Knights
by Sir James Knowles *(cont.)*

But no sooner was Merlin brought before the king than he asked in a vociferous voice, "For what cause was I thus dragged there?"

"My magicians," retorted Vortigern, "told me to seek out a man that had no human father, and to sprinkle my castle with his blood, that it may stand."

"Order those magicians," replied Merlin, "to come before me, and I will convict them of a lie."

The king was astonished at his words, but commanded the magicians to come and sit down before Merlin, who cried to them—

"Because ye know not what it is that hinders the foundation of the castle, ye have advised my blood for a cement to it, as if that would avail, but tell me now rather what there is below that ground, for something there is surely underneath that will not allow the tower to stand?"

The wizards at these words began to tremble with fear, and made no reply. Then said Merlin to the king—"I pray, Lord, that workmen may be ordered to dig deep down into the ground till they shall come to a great pool of water."

This then was done, and the pool discovered far beneath the surface of the ground.

Then, turning again to the magicians, Merlin said, "Tell me now, false sycophants, what there is underneath that pool?"—but again they were silent. Then said he to the king, "Command this pool to be drained, and at the bottom shall be found two dragons, great and huge, which now are sleeping, but which at night awake and fight and tear each other. At their great struggle all the ground shakes and trembles, and so casts down thy towers, which, therefore, never yet could find secure foundations."

The king was amazed at these words, but commanded the pool to be forthwith drained. Surely at the bottom of it did they presently discover the two dragons, fast asleep, as Merlin had declared. Vortigern sat upon the brink of the pool till night to see what else would happen.

Then those two dragons, one of which was white, the other red, rose up and came near one another, and began a sore fight, casting forth fire with their breath. The white dragon had the advantage, and chased the other to the end of the lake where, for grief at his flight, the red dragon turned back upon his foe, renewing

Excerpt from Chapter 1,
King Arthur and His Knights
by Sir James Knowles *(cont.)*

the combat and forcing him to retire in turn. But in the end the red dragon was worsted, and the white dragon disappeared to some unknown destination.

When their battle was done, the king desired Merlin to tell him what it meant. Whereat he, bursting into tears, cried out this prophecy, which first foretold the coming of King Arthur.

"Woe to the red dragon, which symbolizes the British nation, for his banishment cometh quickly. His lurking holes shall be seized by the resilient white dragon—the Saxon whom thou, O king, hast called to the land. The mountains shall be levelled as the valleys, and the rivers of the valleys shall flow with the blood of many men. Cities shall be scorched and churches laid in ruins until at length the oppressed shall turn for a season and prevail against the strangers. For a Boar of Cornwall shall arise and rend them, trampling their necks beneath his feet. The island shall be subject to his power, and he shall take the forests of Gaul. The house of Romulus shall dread him, all the world shall fear him, and no man shall know his end. He shall be immortal in the mouths of the people, and his works shall be food to those that tell them."

#51449—TDQs: Strategies for Building Text-Dependent Questions

© *Shell Education*

Name: _____ Date: _____

Excerpt from Chapter 1,
King Arthur and His Knights
by Sir James Knowles *(cont.)*

Directions: Use the text to answer the questions below.

1 What emotions does King Vortigern experience in the third paragraph? How did you infer what he was feeling without the author stating it explicitly? Reference specific examples from the text to support your answer.

_____

_____

_____

_____

2 In the sentence, "He asked them what these things might be and how one might overcome them," what do the words "things" and "them" refer to? Why is it important to know this to understand the sentence?

_____

_____

_____

_____

3 What inferences can you make from Merlin's dialogue? What evidence from the text supports these inferences?

_____

_____

_____

_____

4 What is the reader expected to infer from the figurative language in the last paragraph? Justify your answer with specific examples from the text.

_____

_____

_____

_____

Excerpt from

Origin and Development of Form and Ornament in Ceramic Art
by William H. Holmes

Forms Suggested by Accident

In the early stages of art, forms suggested by accident are often adopted. These accidental suggestions then become important sources of improvement and progress. This is how the use of clay was discovered and the ceramic art came into existence. The accidental indentation of a mass of clay by a foot, hand, stone, or shell, may have suggested the making of a cup, the simplest form of vessel.

The use of clay as cement in repairing utensils or in building up the walls of shallow vessels may also have led to the formation of disks or cups. It is possible that these shapes then began to be independently constructed. In any case, the objects or utensils used with the clay would impress their forms upon it. Thus, if clay were used in deepening or mending vessels of stone by a given people, it would, when used independently by that people, tend to assume shapes suggested by stone vessels. The same may be said of its use in connection with vessels of other materials. These forms may be said to have an accidental origin, yet they are essentially copies, and may also fall under the next section regarding imitation.

Forms Derived by Imitation

The pliable nature of clay does not impose a given form or class of forms upon its products, as do wood, bark, bone, or stone. It is so supple that it is quite free to take form from its surroundings. In order to investigate the origins of form in early pottery, we must consider the processes by which an art inherits or acquires the forms of another art or of nature. We must also observe how one material imposes its peculiarities upon another material. The primitive artist does not deliberately and freely examine all departments of nature or art and select for models those things most convenient or most agreeable to fancy. Neither does he experiment with the view of inventing new forms. What he attempts depends almost absolutely upon what happens to be suggested by preceding forms.

At first, the range of models in early ceramic art is very limited, and includes only utensils devoted to a particular use. Later, closely-associated objects and utensils are copied. In the first stages of art, when the primitive artist makes a weapon, he modifies or copies a weapon; when he makes a vessel, he modifies or copies a vessel. These originals that the artist imitates may be of two different types: natural or artificial.

Natural originals—There are many different types of original vessels found in nature. These originals differ by country and the climate of origin. The gourd is probably the most varied and suggestive natural vessel. We find that the primitive potter has often copied it in the most literal manner.

Excerpt from

Origin and Development of Form and Ornament in Ceramic Art

by William H. Holmes *(cont.)*

Coastal nations, and those containing large rivers, often use shells of mollusks as efficient receptacles for water and food. Imitations of these are frequently found among the products of the potter's art. In Africa, and in other countries, natural objects such as coconut shells and ostrich eggs are used in a similar manner. Vessels made from the skins, bladders, and stomachs of animals should also be mentioned in this connection. These vessels influenced the formation of earthen utensils too.

Therefore, we find that most of the natural influence for these primitive ceramic forms comes from these objects that were available to be used as vessels at the time. True, other objects have also been copied. We do find many complex natural forms, both animal and vegetable, embodied in vessels of clay. Their presence, however, is indicative of a somewhat advanced stage of art. Over time, the copying of functional vessels gave rise to a familiarity with clay and a capacity in handling it. Eventually, as culture advanced, all nature became within the reach of the potter.

Artificial originals—In most cultures, art had produced vessels in other materials before the use of clay. These vessels were legitimate models for the potter. Therefore, we may expect to find these forms repeated in earthenware. In this way, ceramics acquired many new forms, some of which may have resulted from the natural form of the original material, such as wood or stone. For example, a nation having stone vessels, like those of California, would use these vessels as models for pottery. Forms such as those in Fig. 466 would arise, *a* being in stone and *b* in clay, the former from California and the latter from Arizona.

Similar forms would just as readily come from gourds, baskets, or other utensils. Nations having wooden vessels would copy them in clay upon acquiring the art of pottery. This would give rise to a distinct group of forms, the result primarily of the peculiarities of the woody structure, such as those in Fig. 467.

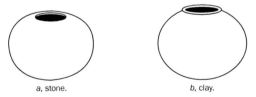

a, stone.   b, clay.

Fig. 466.—Form derived from a stone pot.

a, wood.   b, clay.

Fig. 467.—Form derived from a wooden tray.

Name: _____   Date: _____

Excerpt from
Origin and Development of Form and Ornament in Ceramic Art
by William H. Holmes *(cont.)*

Directions: Use the text to answer the questions below.

1 What does the author already expect you to know about clay in the first paragraph? How do you know? Refer to specific examples from the text to justify your answer.

_____

_____

_____

_____

_____

_____

2 In the third paragraph, the author says, "The pliable nature of clay does not impose a given form or class of forms upon its products, as do wood, bark, bone, or stone." What does this mean? What general knowledge did you use to make this inference?

_____

_____

_____

_____

_____

_____

Excerpt from
Origin and Development of Form and Ornament in Ceramic Art
by William H. Holmes *(cont.)*

3 Reread the sixth paragraph. What do you know explicitly from this paragraph? What personal knowledge do you incorporate to make an inference about the use of early ceramic vessels?

_____

_____

_____

_____

_____

_____

_____

4 What is the purpose of the sentence "Eventually, as culture advanced, all nature became within the reach of the potter"? How does this sentence help you make inferences about the role of nature in the development of ceramics?

_____

_____

_____

_____

_____

_____

_____

Central Ideas and Key Details

Text-dependent questions (TDQs) are important to the understanding of central ideas and key details. In this section, you will find an overview, sample text-dependent questions/prompts, literary and informational passages, as well as supporting questions/prompts to use with your students. Below is a chart that provides the titles and the recommended grade ranges for the texts in this section.

Grade Range	Literary Text	Page #	Informational Text	Page #
K–1	*Friends*	61	*Deserts*	63
2–3	"My Treasures" from *Child's Garden of Verses* by Robert Louis Stevenson	65	*Measuring the Length of Objects*	67
4–5	"The Wise Monkey and the Boar" from *Japanese Fairy Tales* compiled by Yei Theodora Ozaki	70	Excerpt from *Max Planck: Uncovering the World of Matter* by Jane Weir	74
6–8	Excerpt from *Hamlet*, Act IV, Scene VII by William Shakespeare	77	*World War II*	80
9–12	Excerpt from *The Scarlet Letter* by Nathaniel Hawthorne	83	*What Are Cells?*	86

Central Ideas and Key Details Overview

Students need to gain a deep comprehension of the broad themes or central ideas of a text through reading. In order to accomplish this, they also must acquire a general understanding of the literal information and the key details that support these ideas before they can comprehend the larger, overarching messages in the text. In the previous section, we saw how text-dependent questions can be used to understand the role that inference plays in creating text cohesion and combining textual evidence and background knowledge. In this chapter, we will explore how text-dependent questions can serve as guides to facilitate the inference of central ideas and themes from the supporting details in the text.

While some authors may choose to state the central theme of their work explicitly in the text, many authors, especially authors of literature, require the reader to infer the themes without ever stating them directly. As a result, text-dependent questions play a particularly important role in helping students learn to accurately identify the main ideas in a text. By consistently directing students back to the text for verification of their ideas, text-dependent questions enable students to identify the origins of these themes and evaluate the role of these central messages in the text.

In addition to helping students identify and understand the central ideas of a text, text-dependent questions also support comprehension of key details. According to Fisher, Frey, and Alfaro (2013), text-dependent questions about key details help students to "determine the importance of ideas, find supporting details, or answer *who, what, when, where, why, how many,* or *how much*" within the text (128). This foundation then facilitates a deeper and more accurate understanding of central ideas and theme in the text.

In the Common Core State Standards (2010), Reading Anchor Standard 2 specifically states that students should be able to, "determine central ideas or themes of a text and analyze their development" and also "summarize the key supporting details and ideas."

The use of text-dependent questions facilitates this type of analysis at the sentence, paragraph, and comprehensive text level. In the lower grades, this standard is addressed through recounting short stories and texts, including key details. As students' thinking and skill levels advance, they learn how to identify central themes and objectively describe how these ideas develop throughout the text using supporting details. Eventually students learn to analyze the development and interaction of two or more central ideas through key details within complex texts. Throughout this learning process, text-dependent questions offer an effective and engaging way to help students identify key details, recognize important themes and central ideas, and examine the way these literary components interact within fiction and informational texts.

Text-Dependent Questions/Prompts

Summarize/Retell

- Summarize the story by recounting specific key details from the text.

- Retell the story using your own words. Refer back to the text to validate the details included in your retelling of the story.

- What happens in the story? What are the important details? Include specific examples from the text in your answer.

- Retell what happened in the play. Refer back to the text to verify the key details.

- Retell the poem in your own words. Include specific details from the text in your retelling.

- Summarize each stanza of the poem. Include the key details from the poem.

- Summarize the text. What is the central topic? What are the key details that support this topic in the text?

- Summarize the _____ paragraph. What are the key details in the paragraph?

- Summarize page _____. Include key details from the text in your summary.

Main Idea/Theme

- What is the main idea of the story? What details support this idea?

- What is the main idea on page _____? What specific details from the text support your answer?

- What is the theme of the text? How do you know? Include specific information from the text to support your answer.

- What is the main idea of the _____ paragraph? What key details from the text support this idea?

- What is the main idea of each paragraph on page _____? How do these ideas come together to form a central message? Support your answer with specific information from the text.

- What is the focus of the _____ paragraph? How does this focus relate to the overall message of the text? Include specific examples from the text to support your answer.

- What is the theme of the passage? How does the genre of the text play a role in how this theme is communicated to the reader?

- What is the main idea of the text? Where in the text did you find this information?

- How does the author communicate the main idea of the text? Include specific examples from the text to support your answer.

- What is the central idea of the text? How does the author develop this idea over the course of the text?

Text-Dependent Questions/Prompts *(cont.)*

- What is the main thing that you learned from the text? What evidence from the text supports this idea?

- What is the lesson that the author wants you to learn from the story? How does the author communicate this lesson to the reader? Use details from the text to support your answer.

- What is the moral of the story? How do you know?

- How do the characters' actions contribute to the theme of the text? Remember to include specific examples from the text to support your answer.

- How does the author use dialogue to create a theme in the text? Refer back to the text for specific information to justify your answer.

- How does the setting of the story on page _____, in Chapter _____ relate to the theme in the text?

- How does the author develop the theme of the story through the plot? Include specific examples from the text to support your answer.

- How does culture play a role in the main message of the story? Include specific information from the text to support your answer.

- What are some of the multiple themes in the story? How are these themes interwoven throughout the text? Justify your answer with specific details from the text.

- What is the theme of the text? How does the structure of the text affect the theme?

- What is the main idea of scene _____ in the play? How does this idea relate to the overall theme of the play? Include specific details from the text in your answer.

- What is the main problem or conflict in the story/play? How does this challenge play a role in the theme of the story/play?

- What is the main idea of the poem? How do you know? Refer back to the text of the poem to support your answer.

- How does the structure of the poem affect its theme? Use specific examples from the text in your answer.

- How does the speaker reflect on the central idea of the poem? Include specific details from the poem in your answer.

- What is the author's opinion about _____? What details support this opinion?

- Reread the _____ paragraph. How does the phrase/sentence "_____" relate to the overall message of the text? Use examples from the text to support your answer.

Text-Dependent Questions/Prompts *(cont.)*

Key Details

- How do the key details in the text support the overall theme of the story? Include specific examples from the text to support your answer.

- What are the key details of the plot of the story?

- Describe some of the key details about the characters in the story. How do these details affect your overall understanding of the characters?

- What key details in the text does the author use to describe the setting of the story? How do these details contribute to the overall message of the text?

- What are the key details in the paragraph? What is the central idea that these details support?

- What is the relationship between the key details in the _____ paragraph and the _____ paragraph? Include specific examples from the text in your answer.

- List one key detail from each paragraph in the text. How do these details come together to support the overall theme or central idea?

- Reread the paragraph that starts with "_____." What details support the main topic of the text in this paragraph?

Friends

Ben and Jen are squirrels. They are friends. They like to play hide-and-seek.

"I will hide," said Ben.

"Okay," said Jen, "I will look for you."

Jen counted to ten. Then she started looking. She looked under bushes. She looked behind rocks. She looked up in a tree. She could not find Ben anywhere. Then, she heard a voice.

"Help! I'm stuck!" cried Ben. Jen saw Ben's tail. It was poking out of a hole in the ground. Jen grabbed Ben's tail and tugged. Ben was still stuck. Jen pulled harder. Suddenly, Ben flew out of the hole. Jen fell over backwards. They landed in a pile together. They laughed and laughed.

Then, they said, "Let's play again!"

Name: _____ Date: _____

Friends (cont.)

Directions: Use the text to answer the questions below.

1 Summarize the story by writing key details from the text.

_____

- - - - - - - - - - - - - - - -

_____

_____

- - - - - - - - - - - - - - - -

_____

_____

- - - - - - - - - - - - - - - -

_____

_____

- - - - - - - - - - - - - - - -

_____

2 What is the main idea of the story? What details from the text support this idea?

_____

- - - - - - - - - - - - - - - -

_____

_____

- - - - - - - - - - - - - - - -

_____

_____

- - - - - - - - - - - - - - - -

_____

Deserts

Deserts are interesting places. They get very little rain. The ground is dry.

Deserts are mostly sand and dirt. Few plants can grow there.

Cacti grow in the desert. They do not need much water.

A cactus can store water. It holds water in its stem. It can store water for a long time.

Cacti also have long roots. These roots get water from the ground.

Many animals live in the desert.

Foxes build dens in caves and logs. Tortoises make burrows.

Lizards hide under rocks. Snakes live in holes. Owls hunt for mice.

There are many living things in the desert.

Name: _____ Date: _____

Deserts (cont.)

Directions: Use the text to answer the questions below.

1 Summarize the second paragraph. What are the key details?

_____

- - - - - - - - - - - - - - - -

_____
_____

- - - - - - - - - - - - - - - -

_____
_____

- - - - - - - - - - - - - - - -

_____

2 What is the main thing that you learned from the text? What evidence from the text supports this?

_____

- - - - - - - - - - - - - - - -

_____
_____

- - - - - - - - - - - - - - - -

_____
_____

- - - - - - - - - - - - - - - -

_____

"My Treasures" from
Child's Garden of Verses
by Robert Louis Stevenson

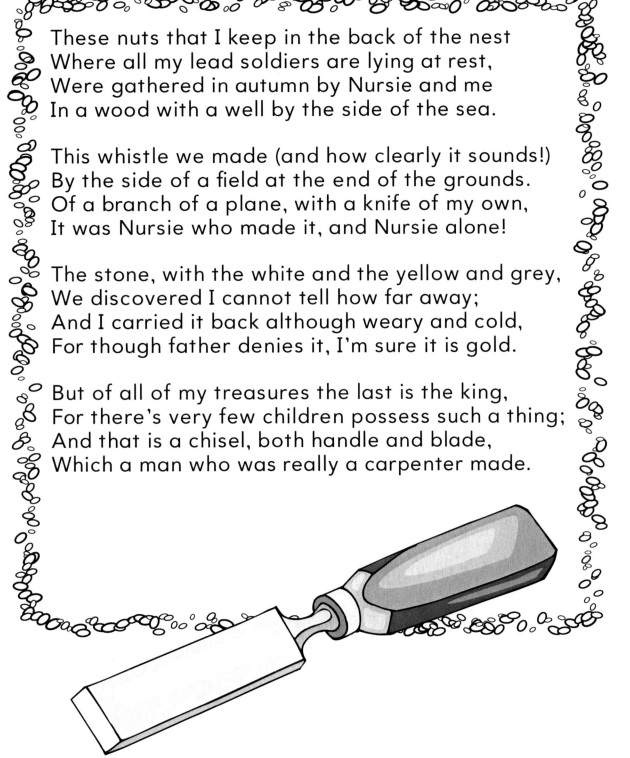

These nuts that I keep in the back of the nest
Where all my lead soldiers are lying at rest,
Were gathered in autumn by Nursie and me
In a wood with a well by the side of the sea.

This whistle we made (and how clearly it sounds!)
By the side of a field at the end of the grounds.
Of a branch of a plane, with a knife of my own,
It was Nursie who made it, and Nursie alone!

The stone, with the white and the yellow and grey,
We discovered I cannot tell how far away;
And I carried it back although weary and cold,
For though father denies it, I'm sure it is gold.

But of all of my treasures the last is the king,
For there's very few children possess such a thing;
And that is a chisel, both handle and blade,
Which a man who was really a carpenter made.

Name: _____   Date: _____

"My Treasures" from
Child's Garden of Verses
by Robert Louis Stevenson *(cont.)*

Directions: Use the text to answer the questions below.

1 Summarize the second stanza. What are the key details?

_____

_____

_____

_____

2 What is the main idea of the poem? How do you know? Refer back to the text to support your answer.

_____

_____

_____

_____

3 What are some of the key details in the poem? How do these details support the main topic of the poem?

_____

_____

_____

_____

#51449—TDQs: Strategies for Building Text-Dependent Questions   © Shell Education

Measuring the Length of Objects

Is your foot really a foot long? How many inches is your hand? How many millimeters is a paper clip? There are many ways to measure the length of things.

Length is the measure of a thing from one end to the other end. There are many tools used to measure length. But most of the time we use a ruler. Yardsticks and meter sticks can be used, too. Many people even use tape measures to measure length.

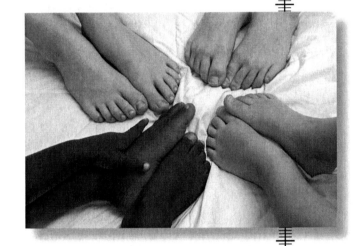

Length Units of Measurement

There are a lot of units you can use to measure length. In the United States, we use English units of measurement. But, in many other countries, they use the metric system.

English Units	Metric Units
inches	millimeters
feet	centimeters
yards	meters
miles	kilometers

Measuring the Length of Objects (cont.)

So How Long Is It?

How long is an inch? An inch is about as wide as two fingers. Some say the inch was the width of a king's thumb. But we do not know the true story. An inchworm is about an inch long. So is a small paper clip. One inch is 2.54 centimeters.

A yard is used to measure length. A yard is three feet. It is 36 inches. Many say that Henry I of England made the yard. It was the length from the tip of his nose to the tip of his finger when his arms were out. It is easier to measure long things with a yardstick. A football field is measured in yards. It is 100 yards long. A yard is very close to a metric meter.

A mile is a large unit used to measure length. A mile is 5,280 feet. The Romans were the first to use a mile. They measured it using steps. Their steps equaled 5,000 feet. That made their mile. When you go on a trip, you measure the distance in miles. Running tracks are a quarter-mile long. A mile is close to a kilometer. One mile is 1.6 kilometers.

Name: _____ Date: _____

Measuring the Length of Objects (cont.)

Directions: Use the text to answer the questions below.

1 Summarize the second paragraph. What are the key details in the paragraph?

_____

_____

_____

_____

2 What is the focus of the last paragraph? How does this focus relate to the overall message of the text? Include specific examples from the text to support your answer.

_____

_____

_____

_____

3 List one key detail from each paragraph in the text. How do these details come together to create an overall theme or central idea?

_____

_____

_____

_____

"The Wise Monkey and the Boar"
from *Japanese Fairy Tales*
compiled by Yei Theodora Ozaki

Long, long ago, there lived in the province of Shinshin in Japan, a traveling monkey-man, who earned his living by taking round a monkey and showing off the animal's tricks. One evening the man came home in a very bad temper and told his wife to send for the butcher the next morning. The wife was very bewildered and asked her husband, "Why do you wish me to send for the butcher?"

"The monkey's too old and forgets his tricks. I must now sell him to the butcher."

The woman felt very sorry for the poor little animal, and pleaded for her husband to spare him, but her pleading was all in vain. Now the monkey was in the next room and he soon understood that he was to be killed, and he said to himself, "Here I have served him faithfully, and he is going to send me to the butcher? What am I to do?!"

There was no time to lose. The monkey slipped out of the house and ran as quickly as he could to the nearby forest to find the wise boar. He found the boar and began his tale of woe at once.

"Good Mr. Boar, I have heard of your excellent wisdom. I am in great trouble, you alone can help me. I have grown old in the service of my master, and because I cannot dance properly now he intends to sell me to the butcher. What do you advise me to do? I know how clever you are!"

The boar was pleased at the flattery. He thought for a little while and then said, "Hasn't your master a baby?"

"Oh, yes," said the monkey, "he has one infant son."

"I will come round early tomorrow morning and I will seize the child and run off with it. The mother will have a tremendous scare, and before your master and mistress know what to do, you must run

"The Wise Monkey and the Boar"

from *Japanese Fairy Tales*
compiled by Yei Theodora Ozaki *(cont.)*

after me and rescue the child and take it home safely to its parents, and you will see that when the butcher comes they won't have the heart to sell you."

The monkey thanked the boar many times and then went home. The next morning, the mother placed her child near the porch. Suddenly there was a noise in the porch and a loud cry from the child. When the man and his wife arrived outside, they saw the boar disappearing with the child in its clutch and the monkey running after the thief as hard as his legs would carry him.

Both the man and wife admired the courageous conduct of the wise monkey. Their gratitude knew no bounds when the faithful monkey brought the child safely back to their arms.

"There!" said the wife. "This is the animal you want to kill—if the monkey hadn't been here we should have lost our child forever."

"You are right, wife, for once," said the man as he carried the child into the house. "You may send the butcher back when he comes."

When the butcher arrived he was sent away with an order for some boar's meat for the evening dinner, and the monkey was petted and lived the rest of his days in peace.

Name: _____ Date: _____

"The Wise Monkey and the Boar"

from *Japanese Fairy Tales*
compiled by Yei Theodora Ozaki *(cont.)*

Directions: Use the text to answer the questions below.

1 Retell the story. What culture does this story come from? How does culture affect the telling of the story?

_____

_____

_____

_____

_____

2 What is the moral of the story? How do you know?

_____

_____

_____

_____

"The Wise Monkey and the Boar"

from *Japanese Fairy Tales*
compiled by Yei Theodora Ozaki *(cont.)*

3 What is the main problem or conflict in the story? How does this challenge play a role in the theme of the story? Use evidence from the story to support your answer.

_____

_____

_____

_____

_____

4 What are the key details in the paragraph that starts with "Good Mr. Boar..."? What is the central idea that these details support?

_____

_____

_____

_____

Excerpt from

Max Planck: Uncovering the World of Matter

by Jane Weir

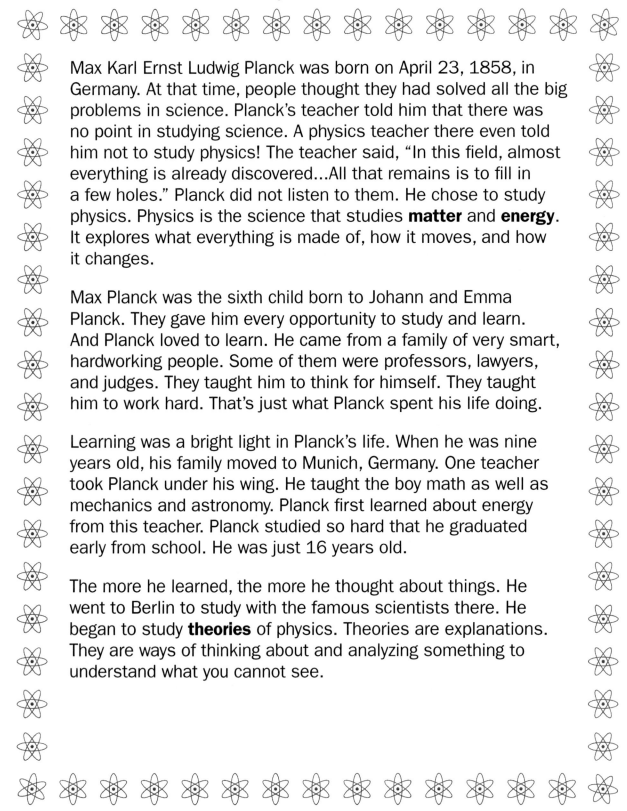

Max Karl Ernst Ludwig Planck was born on April 23, 1858, in Germany. At that time, people thought they had solved all the big problems in science. Planck's teacher told him that there was no point in studying science. A physics teacher there even told him not to study physics! The teacher said, "In this field, almost everything is already discovered...All that remains is to fill in a few holes." Planck did not listen to them. He chose to study physics. Physics is the science that studies **matter** and **energy**. It explores what everything is made of, how it moves, and how it changes.

Max Planck was the sixth child born to Johann and Emma Planck. They gave him every opportunity to study and learn. And Planck loved to learn. He came from a family of very smart, hardworking people. Some of them were professors, lawyers, and judges. They taught him to think for himself. They taught him to work hard. That's just what Planck spent his life doing.

Learning was a bright light in Planck's life. When he was nine years old, his family moved to Munich, Germany. One teacher took Planck under his wing. He taught the boy math as well as mechanics and astronomy. Planck first learned about energy from this teacher. Planck studied so hard that he graduated early from school. He was just 16 years old.

The more he learned, the more he thought about things. He went to Berlin to study with the famous scientists there. He began to study **theories** of physics. Theories are explanations. They are ways of thinking about and analyzing something to understand what you cannot see.

Excerpt from
Max Planck: Uncovering the World of Matter
by Jane Weir *(cont.)*

Planck studied matter and its properties. This led him to learn what happens to matter in different conditions. Matter and heat really interested him. All of Planck's studies led him to choose heat theory as his field. He would go on to make big discoveries about matter and heat.

As time went on, Planck found he didn't want to do experiments anymore. He wanted to explain why things are as they are. He took what was known and used it to help understand what wasn't known. He proved there was a whole lot left to learn in science. It's a good thing Planck didn't listen. The twentieth century turned out to be very busy for scientists. And a lot of new things were learned because of Planck!

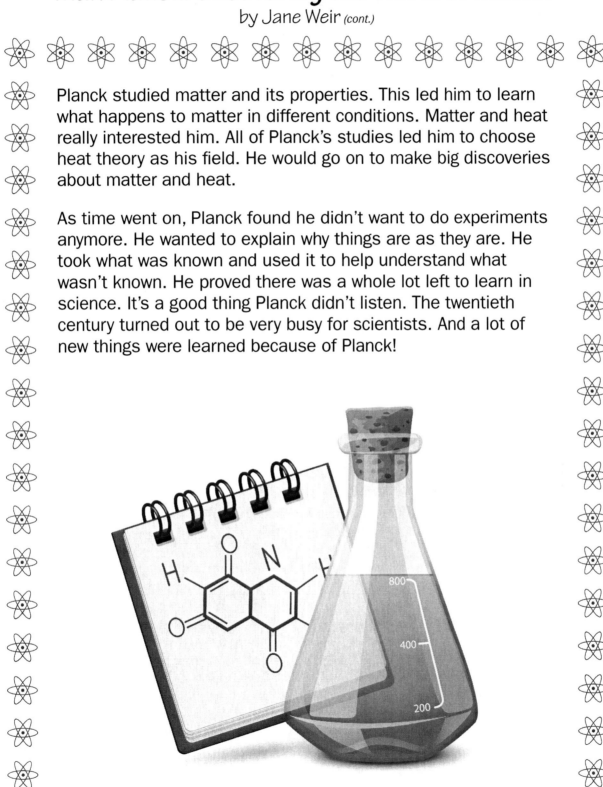

Name: _____ Date: _____

Excerpt from

Max Planck: Uncovering the World of Matter
by Jane Weir *(cont.)*

Directions: Use the text to answer the questions below.

1 Summarize the third paragraph. What are the key details in the paragraph?

_____

_____

_____

2 What is the central idea of the text? How does the author develop this idea over the course of the text?

_____

_____

_____

3 Reread the first paragraph. How does the sentence "A physics teacher there even told him not to study physics!" relate to the overall message of the text? Use examples from the text to support your answer.

_____

_____

_____

4 What is the purpose of the details in the fourth paragraph? Use examples from the text to justify your opinion.

_____

_____

_____

Excerpt from
Hamlet, Act IV, Scene VII
by William Shakespeare

King Claudius:	There should be no place in the world that allows murder, but revenge is not murder; revenge is different and should have no rules and no boundaries. If you want revenge on Hamlet for killing your father, come close and listen, because I have a plan. Hamlet knows you have just returned home from school so I will praise you in front of him, and I will tell him of all of the wonderful things you learned while in school. This will make Hamlet jealous of you and, playing on this jealousy, I will suggest that you and Hamlet have a fight with swords. I will say that it will be to showcase the skills you learned while you were away at school, and Hamlet will agree so that he can lessen his own feelings of guilt. I will make it known to everyone that no one will be hurt in this pretend fight, but secretly, you and I will know the true intention of the duel: Hamlet's death. We will put poison on the tip of your sword so you will not have to hurt Hamlet outwardly. All you will have to do is prick the sword's tip against his arm and you will have your revenge for your father.
Laertes:	I will do it, for while I was at school, I found some strong poison that is so dangerous that just a drop of it will kill a man. It is this poison that will sharpen the tip of my sword.
King Claudius:	But we have to ensure that this plan does not fail, so I have another way we can guarantee Hamlet's death. At the start of the fight, I will pour a cup of wine for Hamlet, toast to show my support for Hamlet to the people, and then drop a poisoned pearl into the cup. Everyone in the palace will think I am doing it to honor Hamlet. Then when Hamlet is tired and out of breath, he will drink from the cup, and that will ensure that he does not make it out alive.

Enter Queen Gertrude

My lovely queen! What is the matter?

Excerpt from
Hamlet, Act IV, Scene VII
by William Shakespeare *(cont.)*

Queen Gertrude: One sorrowful event seems to bring about another sorrowful event. Laertes, your sister, Ophelia, is drowned.

Laertes: Drowned! Where? How?

Queen Gertrude: Ophelia sat down by the creek and began to make herself a crown of soft and beautiful flowers. Once she had dressed herself with her flowery creations, she went to the side of the creek to see her reflection in the glassy water, but when she leaned over, she lost her balance and tumbled into the water. In the silent water, she found her death.

Laertes: How can that be?

Queen Gertrude: She is drowned.

Laertes: Your death already has too much water, beautiful Ophelia, so I will not cry watery tears in my sadness, but instead I will take revenge for your premature death—our death and the death of our father.

Name: _____ Date: _____

Excerpt from
Hamlet, Act IV, Scene VII
by William Shakespeare *(cont.)*

Directions: Use the text to answer the questions below.

1 Retell what happened in the play. Refer back to the text to verify the key details.

_____

_____

_____

_____

2 What is the theme of the scene? How does the structure of the text affect the theme?

_____

_____

_____

_____

3 How does the author develop the theme of the story through the plot? Include specific examples from the text to support your answer.

_____

_____

_____

_____

4 Describe some of the key details about the characters in the story. How do these details affect your overall understanding of the characters?

_____

_____

_____

_____

World War II

How the War Began

Adolf Hitler was the leader of **Nazi** Germany and he wanted to make Germany bigger. In 1938, he announced a plan to merge his homeland of Austria with Germany. Soon, Nazi flags flew all over Austria.

Then, Hitler decided to take over Czechoslovakia. He printed lies in German newspapers saying that Germans were treated badly in that country. He reminded Germans that before World War I, Czechoslovakia was part of Germany. No one objected, so his army took over that country, too.

Hitler wanted to take over all of Europe, and it seemed the world was going to let him do it. He planned to attack Poland next, but this time, both Great Britain and France objected. They warned him that this would start a war, but Hitler believed they would not stop him.

On September 1, 1939, Hitler invaded Poland, and World War II began. Hitler destroyed the Polish capital. He hoped that this easy victory would scare the British and French. Hitler offered them a chance for peace, but they refused. This time, Hitler had gone too far, and Britain and France were not going to let him get away with it.

How the United States Got Involved

December 7, 1941, started out like any other quiet Sunday in Hawaii. People were getting out of bed and starting their days. Suddenly, their world changed forever. Hundreds of Japanese airplanes started bombing the U.S. military base at Pearl Harbor. The terrible surprise attack lasted for almost two hours. More than 2,400 people were killed and almost 1,200 more were wounded.

Before this day, the war in Europe seemed far away to people in the United States. But World War II was not just fought in Europe. There was now an enemy in the Pacific, too. When the Japanese attacked Pearl Harbor that day, it shocked the world.

For Americans, this day pushed them into the deadly war both with Japan and Europe. For the world, it sparked the beginning of a nuclear era. Scientists created bombs that destroyed entire cities and spared no one, including innocent children. World War II was an ugly, vicious war.

World War II *(cont.)*

Why Stay Out of the War?

People today may wonder why the United States stayed out of the war at first. Why were they not alarmed when dictators like Hitler came to power? In fact, many Americans were alarmed by these dictators, but some leaders in Congress felt the United States should stay out of all wars. These people were pacifists. They felt that their good example would encourage others to support peace. Others felt the United States should keep to itself because they did not want to get involved in another European war. They were known as isolationists and they did not think it was important to keep a strong military. However, President Franklin Roosevelt disagreed. He knew he had to build up the military. He was not about to let dictators take over his free country. In the end, Hitler and the Japanese were defeated. But it was at the expense of many lives. Many hope that we will never have a war like that again!

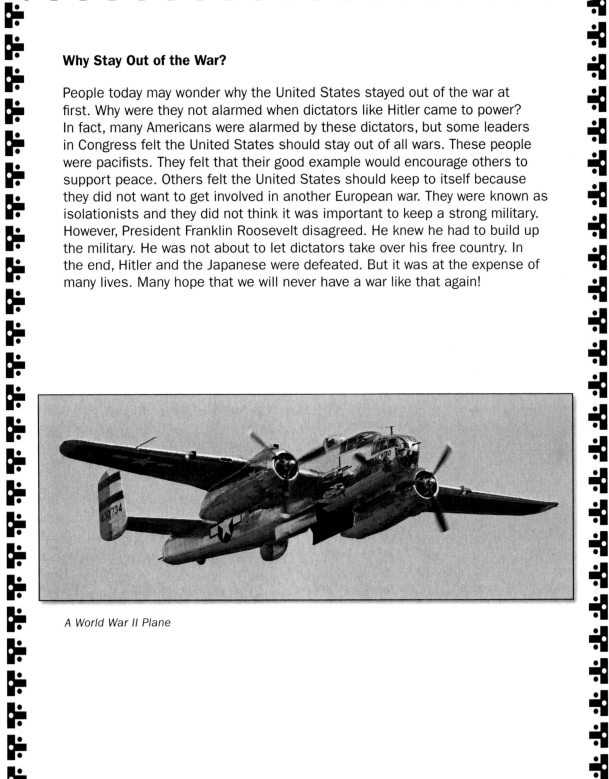

A World War II Plane

Name: _____ Date: _____

World War II (cont.)

Directions: Use the text to answer the questions below.

1 What is the main thing that you learned from the text? What evidence from the text supports this?

_____

_____

_____

_____

2 Reread the third paragraph. How does the sentence "Hitler wanted to take over all of Europe, and it seemed the world was going to let him do it" relate to the overall message of the text? Use examples from the text to support your answer.

_____

_____

_____

_____

3 List some of the key details from the text. Refer back to the text for specific information about these details.

_____

_____

_____

_____

4 What is the focus of the fifth paragraph? How does this focus relate to the overall message of the text? Include specific examples from the text to support your answer.

_____

_____

_____

_____

Excerpt from
The Scarlet Letter
by Nathaniel Hawthorne

It was a circumstance to be noted on the summer morning when our story begins its course, that the women, of whom there were several in the crowd, appeared to take a peculiar interest in whatever penal infliction might be expected to ensue. The age had not so much refinement that any sense of impropriety restrained these women from wedging themselves into the throng nearest to the scaffold at an execution. Morally, as well as materially, there was a coarser fiber in those wives and maidens of old English birth and breeding than in their fair descendants. For, throughout that chain of ancestry, every successive mother had transmitted to her child a more delicate and briefer beauty, and a slighter physical frame, if not character of less force and solidity than her own. The women who were now standing about the prison-door stood within less than half a century of the period when the man-like Elizabeth had been the not altogether unsuitable representative of the sex. They were her countrywomen. The beef and ale of their native land, with a moral diet not a whit more refined, entered largely into their composition. The bright morning sun, therefore, shone on broad shoulders and well-developed busts, and on round and ruddy cheeks, that had ripened in the far-off island, and had hardly yet grown paler or thinner in the atmosphere of New England. There was, moreover, a boldness and rotundity of speech among these matrons that would startle us at the present day, whether in respect to its purport or its volume of tone.

"Goodwives," said a hard-featured dame of fifty, "I'll tell ye a piece of my mind. It would be greatly for the public benefit if we women, being of mature age and church-members in good repute, should have the handling of such criminal as this Hester Prynne. What think ye, gossips? If the hussy stood up for judgment before us five, would she come off with such a sentence as the worshipful magistrates have awarded? I think not."

"People say," said another, "that the Reverend Master Dimmesdale, her godly pastor, is very grieved that such a scandal should have come upon his congregation."

"The magistrates are God-fearing gentlemen, but merciful overmuch. That is the truth," added a third autumnal matron. "At the very least, they should have put the brand of a hot iron on Hester Prynne's forehead. Madame Hester would have winced at that, I warrant me. But she—the naughty baggage—little will she care what they put upon the bodice of her gown! Why, look you, she may cover it with a brooch, or such like heathenish adornment, and so walk the streets as brave as ever!"

"Ah, but," interposed, more softly, a young wife, holding a child by the hand, "let her cover the mark as she will, the pang of it will be always in her heart."

Excerpt from
The Scarlet Letter
by Nathaniel Hawthorne *(cont.)*

"What do we talk of marks and brands, whether on the bodice of her gown or the flesh of her forehead?" cried another female, the ugliest as well as the most pitiless of these self-constituted judges. "This woman has brought shame upon us all, and ought to die. Is there not law for it? Truly there is, both in the Scripture and the statute-book. Then let the magistrates, who have made it of no effect, thank themselves if their own wives and daughters go astray."

"Mercy on us, goodwife!" exclaimed a man in the crowd, "is there no virtue in woman, save what springs from a wholesome fear of the gallows? That is the hardest word yet! Hush now, for the lock is turning in the prison-door. Here comes Mistress Prynne herself."

The door of the jail flung open. From within appeared, like a black shadow emerging into sunshine, the grim and gristly presence of the town-beadle, with a sword by his side, and his staff of office in his hand. This personage prefigured and represented in his aspect the whole dismal severity of the Puritanic code of law. It was his business to administer this law, in its final and closest application, to the offender. Stretching forth the official staff in his left hand, he laid his right upon the shoulder of a young woman. He drew her forward, until, on the threshold of the prison-door, she repelled him, by an action marked with natural dignity and force of character. Then she stepped into the open air as if by her own free will. She bore in her arms a child, a baby of some three months old, who turned aside its little face from the too vivid light of day. The baby's existence, heretofore, had brought it acquaintance only with the grey twilight of a dungeon, or other darksome apartment of the prison.

When the young woman—the mother of this child—stood fully revealed before the crowd, it seemed to be her first impulse to clasp the infant closely to her bosom. This action seemed born not so much by an impulse of motherly affection, but so that she might thereby conceal a certain token, which was wrought or fastened into her dress. In a moment, however, wisely judging that one token of her shame would but poorly serve to hide another, she took the baby on her arm. With a burning blush, and yet a haughty smile, and a glance that would not be abashed, she looked around at her townspeople and neighbors. On the breast of her gown, in fine red cloth, surrounded with elaborate embroidery and fantastic flourishes of gold thread, appeared the letter A. It was so artistically done, and with so much fertility and gorgeous luxuriance of fancy, that it had all the effect of a last and fitting decoration to the apparel which she wore, and which was of a splendor in accordance with the taste of the age, but greatly beyond what was allowed by the sumptuary regulations of the colony.

Name: _____ Date: _____

Excerpt from
The Scarlet Letter
by Nathaniel Hawthorne *(cont.)*

Directions: Use the text to answer the questions below.

1 Provide an objective summary of the text. Include examples from the text, not your personal opinions or judgments.

_____

_____

_____

_____

2 What is the theme of the text? How do you know? Include specific information from the text to support your answer.

_____

_____

_____

_____

3 How does the author use dialogue to create a theme in the text? Refer back to the text for specific information to justify your answer.

_____

_____

_____

_____

4 What key details does the author use to describe the setting of the story? How do these details contribute to the overall message of the text?

_____

_____

_____

_____

What Are Cells?

Every living thing is comprised of cells. Some **organisms**, such as an amoeba or a bacterium, are just one cell. However, most organisms are **multicellular**, which means they are comprised of many cells. Humans, animals, and plants are all examples of multicellular organisms.

Multicellular things can be made of trillions of cells that all work together and help the organism do many things such as eat, create energy, get rid of waste, reproduce, and even make new cells. Cells communicate with one another by exchanging tiny chemical messages. These chemical messages move molecules from place to place and thousands of these reactions take place in your body every second.

DNA

You probably know that DNA is the instruction manual for building your body, but how does it work? DNA is in every cell; it is the "brain" behind cell operation. DNA is a long, stringy molecule that contains the alleles that tell the cell when to make different proteins. Every gene contains two alleles and the cell follows instructions from both sets of alleles simultaneously. If both alleles tell the cell to make a certain protein, the cell may make a lot of this particular protein. On the other hand, if the alleles instruct the cell to make distinct proteins, then the cell will follow the directions. Whatever the result, the pair of alleles "express" the gene.

The Cell Cycles

The cell cycles are comprised of two phases—the interphase and **mitosis**. A cell is in interphase about 90 percent of the time and then goes into the period of mitosis. Mitosis occurs when the cell divides itself, and then the new cells return to interphase.

Cells are not easily able to divide in half; successful mitosis requires the creation of an exact copy, including their DNA, during interphase to survive and work properly.

Interphase occurs in three phases: G1, S, and G2. In the first phase, G1, the newly formed cell processes all the materials it needs to grow strong, and then it enters into the S-phase. During the S-phase, the DNA makes a copy of itself and these two DNA copies remain linked together at a point called the **centromere**. Interphase ends with the G2-phase where the cell checks to be sure the newly copied DNA is in order before the cell divides.

Cell division, or mitosis, occurs in five phases: prophase, metaphase, anaphase, telophase, and cytokinesis. Together these five phases take about two hours to complete.

Prophase

During **prophase**, the first phase of mitosis, the cell's nuclear membrane first disappears and then the strands of DNA that paired off during interphase thicken. These pairs become short, stubby rods called chromatids. They look like tiny Xs, attached at the center by the centromere, when you view them under a light microscope.

What Are Cells? (cont.)

Metaphase

In the **metaphase**, the second phase of mitosis, the chromosome pairs move to the center, or the equator, of the cell. The pairs line up across the equator, and then protein threads grow from the aster. The centrioles are located at the cell's north and south poles and the centromeres on each chromosome pair are lined up along the equator with threads connecting the centrioles and the centromeres. This new connection is called the spindle and the cell is now ready to divide.

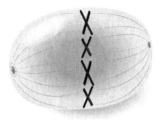

Anaphase

Anaphase is the third phase of mitosis that occurs when the cell signals the protein threads of the spindle to lengthen, making the cell longer, too. The threads pull the chromosomes towards the poles so that each pole now contains a complete set of chromosomes. When the cell divides, each cell will contain a complete set of the same genetic blueprints.

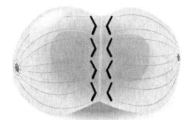

Telophase

Telophase is the fourth and final phase in the process of mitosis. During telophase, the chromosomes finally arrive at the north and south poles of the cells, and they begin to organize themselves into new nuclei. A membrane forms around each new nucleus and the spindle fibers begin to disappear.

Cytokinesis

During **cytokinesis**, the two cells separate fully and each newly formed cell now contains an identical set of genetic information as the parent cell.

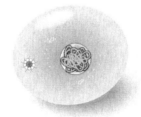
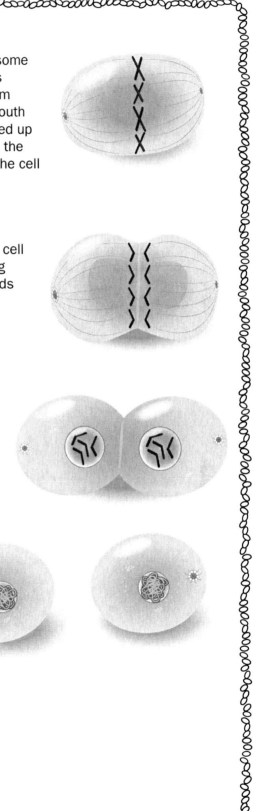

Name: _____ Date: _____

What Are Cells? *(cont.)*

Directions: Use the text to answer the questions below.

1 Summarize the text. What is the central topic? What are the key details that support this topic in the text?

_____

_____

_____

_____

_____

2 Reread the third paragraph. How does the sentence "You probably know that DNA is the recipe for building your body, but how does it work?" relate to the overall message of the text? Use examples from the text to support your answer.

_____

_____

_____

_____

3 What is the relationship between the key details in the seventh paragraph and the eighth paragraph? Be sure to include specific examples from the text in your answer.

_____

_____

_____

_____

4 Reread the paragraph that starts with "Multicellular things…" What details support the main topic of the text in this paragraph?

_____

_____

_____

_____

#51449—TDQs: Strategies for Building Text-Dependent Questions   © *Shell Education*

Individuals, Events, and Ideas

Text-dependent questions (TDQs) are important to the understanding of individuals, events, and ideas. In this section, you will find an overview, sample text-dependent questions/prompts, literary and informational passages, as well as supporting questions/prompts to use with your students. Below is a chart that provides the titles and the recommended grade ranges for the texts in this section.

Grade Range	Literary Text	Page #	Informational Text	Page #
K–1	*The Picky Boy*	95	*Your Sense of Taste*	97
2–3	"The Shoemaker and the Elves" from *The Beacon Second Reader* by James H. Fassett	99	Excerpt from *Solids* by Lisa Greathouse	102
4–5	Excerpt from *The Jungle Book* by Rudyard Kipling	105	Collecting Data	108
6–8	Excerpt from *Call of the Wild* by Jack London	111	Excerpt from *Ancient Rome* by Betsey Norris	113
9–12	Excerpt from Chapter 3, *Pride and Prejudice* by Jane Austen	115	Excerpt from *The Every-Day Life of Abraham Lincoln* by Frances Fisher Browne	118

Individuals, Events, and Ideas Overview

Stories and informational texts generally contain numerous different literary elements, but the foundation of any text comes from the individuals, events, or ideas that make up the body of the writing. In literature, the author interweaves characters, setting, and plot to build theme, create conflict, achieve resolution, and construct a point of view. Informational texts use writing and text structures to convey information about historical events, explain technical procedures, describe scientific procedures, explore significant individuals, and much more. Text-dependent questions that focus on the individuals, events, and ideas contained within a text help students learn to identify these significant components and analyze their development over the course of a text. A thorough understanding of these elements then enables the student to comprehend the broader themes and complex central ideas embedded within the text.

It is important that students not only understand the *who*, *what*, and *where* of a text, but also that they examine why the author chose to develop these fundamental components in specific ways. According to Day and Park (2005), *how* or *why* questions about individuals, locations, and events in a text can be used to help students "go beyond a literal understanding of the text" and aide them in becoming "interactive readers" (66). For example, text-dependent questions can challenge students to examine the text for the reasons *why* characters or individuals act in a given way or *how* a particular setting affects a sequence of events. By looking beyond the literal facts, students realize how these literary components develop and interact.

Reading Anchor Standard 3 in the Common Core (2010) mandates students be able to "analyze how and why individuals, events, or ideas develop and interact over the course of a text." For literary texts in the elementary grades, students begin by learning to identify and describe the characters, setting, and major events. Later, they practice analyzing how the characters interact with particular events as well as comparing and contrasting multiple characters, events, and settings. Similarly, in informational texts, students start by looking at the different ways that individuals, events, ideas, or pieces of information are related. They learn to use language involving sequence, cause and effect, and chronology to examine informational texts. Students explore the ways in which ideas develop over the course of a text and investigate how authors effectively communicate information and opinions to the reader.

In order to successfully analyze and comprehend the contents of a story or informational text, it is important that students explicitly refer to the details and information presented within the text. Text-dependent questions enable students to deepen their comprehension and draw conclusions based on information directly from the text, rather than relying exclusively on ideas based on prior experiences or background knowledge.

Text-Dependent Questions/Prompts

Individuals/Characters

- What did you learn about _____ in the _____ paragraph? What words did the author use to communicate this information?

- What emotions does _____ experience in the text? How do you know?

- What do _____'s actions show you in the _____ page/paragraph/scene/stanza?

- What is the relationship between _____ and _____? Refer back to the text for specific examples to support your answer.

- What are _____'s strengths? Weaknesses? How do you know?

- How does the dialogue between _____ and _____ help the reader understand more about these characters/individuals? Use examples from the text to support your answer.

- What does _____ look like? What words or phrases does the author use to describe him/her?

- What is _____'s motivation in the _____ paragraph/scene/stanza? What words or phrases in the text tell you this?

- What is _____'s emotional state in the _____ paragraph/scene/stanza? How do you know? Use examples from the text to support your answer.

- What problems does _____ face in the text? How does his/her personality affect the outcome of these problems? Refer back to the text in your answer.

- What does the author want the reader to know/understand about _____? How do you know this from the text?

- How does _____ act around _____? What do these actions tell you about the relationship between these two individuals? Support your answer with details from the text.

- How does the author develop the character of _____ over the course of the story? Include specific examples from the text in your answer.

- How does _____ change during the story? Support your answer with specific examples from the text.

- What words does the author use to describe _____? What can you infer about _____ from these words?

- What are _____'s feelings about _____? Include specific words and phrases from the text to support your answer.

- Compare _____ and _____. How are these two characters/individuals alike and different? Refer back to the text for evidence to justify your answer.

- Why does _____ say, "_____"? How does this dialogue relate to _____'s character?

- What is the historical significance of _____? Remember to include examples from the text in your answer.

Text-Dependent Questions/Prompts (cont.)

- What do you learn about _____ in the paragraph that starts with, "_____"?
- Who are the main characters/people in this text? Describe each character/person using details from the text.
- Why is it important to learn about the life of _____? Include examples from the text to justify your opinion.
- What is _____'s role in the text? Why did the author choose to include him/her? Support your answer with textual evidence.

Setting

- What is the setting of the text? Remember to include specific words and phrases from the text in your answer.
- What role does the setting play in the story/text? Include examples from the text to support your answer.
- How does the time at which the text takes place play a role in the story? Support your answer with examples from the text.
- What words does the author use to describe the setting? Be sure to include specific words and phrases from the text in your answer.
- How does the setting affect the overall tone of the text? Why is this important? Use examples from the text to demonstrate the relationship between setting and tone.
- How does setting affect the life of _____? How do you know?
- What is the historical significance of the setting of the story/play/poem/text? Remember to include examples from the text to support your answer.
- How would the story change if it occurred in a different location? Provide evidence from the text to illustrate your answer.
- How is the sequence of events in the text affected by the setting?
- What is the connection between setting and character development in the story? Support your answer with examples from the text.

Events/Plot

- Summarize the sequence of events in the story. Be sure not to include personal opinions or judgments.
- How do the events in chapter _____ relate to those in chapter _____?
- Describe how the events in the text build on each other. Make sure to include specific examples from the text in your answer.
- What is the main event on page _____? What is the role of this event in the overall text?

Text-Dependent Questions/Prompts (cont.)

- Why did _____ happen? Refer back to the text for evidence to support your answer.

- What is the role of _____ in the sequence of events? How do you know?

- Why did the author choose to focus on the events of _____? Justify your answer with specific details from the text.

- Retell the main events of the story. How do these events relate to the overall message of the text?

- Explain the relationship between the sequence of events and character development in the text. Include specific examples from the text in your answer.

- How does the event in paragraph _____ signify a turning point in the text? Refer back to the text for details to support your answer.

- What event comes before _____? Why is this significant?

- What event comes after _____? Describe the role of this sequence in the text.

- Explain how the series of events on page _____ contribute to/support the overall theme of the text. Make sure to include specific examples from the text to support your answer.

- What is one problem/conflict in the text? How is it resolved?

- What is the cause and effect discussed in the text?

- How do the series of events at the beginning of the story contribute to the overall tone of the text? Support your answer with specific examples from the text.

- How does the text's genre relate to the sequence of events in the text? Refer back to the text in your answer.

The Picky Boy

Scott is six years old. He is a very picky boy.

He does not like dogs. He does not like apples. He does not like to run or jump.

Scott does not like the color red or the taste of salt. He hates rainy days and he does not like sunny days either.

He never goes swimming. Scott does not have many friends. His only friend is his cat, Spots.

He spends most of the time by himself and he does not smile very much.

Name: _____ Date: _____

The Picky Boy (cont.)

Directions: Use the text to answer the questions below.

1 What did you learn about Scott in the text? What words did the author use to tell you this?

_____

_____

_____

_____

_____

_____

2 What is the relationship between Scott and Spots? Use an example from the text to support your answer.

_____

_____

_____

_____

_____

_____

Your Sense of Taste

Taste is one of the five senses. You use your tongue to taste things. Your tongue has taste buds. The taste buds figure out the flavor in the food you eat. Foods can taste sweet or salty. They can taste sour or bitter. Some foods can have more than one taste. Lemonade can be sweet and sour at the same time.

When you put food in your mouth, your taste buds send messages to your brain. The way food smells also affects its flavor. When you chew food, it gives out different smells. Your nose smells the food. Then, it sends a signal to your brain. Your brain gets the messages. It puts together the signals from your tongue and nose. That is how your body senses flavor in food.

Some people like sweet food best. Other people like salty food best. Which taste is your favorite?

Name: _____ Date: _____

Your Sense of Taste (cont.)

Directions: Use the text to answer the questions below.

1 What is the purpose of the text? Include examples from the text to support your answer.

_____

_____

_____

_____

_____

_____

_____

_____

_____

_____

2 What examples does the author use to help you understand the concept of taste in the text?

_____

_____

_____

_____

_____

_____

_____

_____

"The Shoemaker and the Elves"
from *The Beacon Second Reader*
by James H. Fassett

A shoemaker and his wife lived in a little house on the edge of a wood. They were very poor, and each day they grew poorer and poorer. At last there was nothing left in the house but leather for one pair of shoes.

"I will cut out this last pair of shoes," the shoemaker said to his wife. "Tomorrow I will sew them."

So he cut out the leather and left it on his bench. The next morning he went into his shop to make the shoes. What did he see? A pair of shoes, all nicely made and ready to be sold. The stitches were so fine and the shoes so well made that they were quickly sold. With the money, the poor shoemaker bought leather for two pairs of shoes. Then he said to his wife, "I will cut out the leather for two pairs of shoes. Tomorrow I will sew them."

So he cut out the leather for the shoes and left it on his bench. The next morning when he went into his shop there were two pairs of shoes already made. The work was so well done that those shoes were also sold very quickly. With the money, the poor shoemaker bought enough leather for four pairs of shoes. Those he also cut out and left upon his bench. The next morning he found four pairs of beautiful shoes, all well made. And so it went on and on. Instead of being a very poor shoemaker, he became a very rich shoemaker. His shoes were so well made that even the queen herself wore them.

At last the shoemaker said to his wife, "We must find out who makes the shoes." So one bright moonlight night they hid behind a curtain where they could watch the bench

"The Shoemaker and the Elves"
from *The Beacon Second Reader*
by James H. Fassett *(cont.)*

and not be seen. Just on the stroke of midnight, two little elves jumped through the window. They went skipping and dancing up to the bench. Sitting cross-legged they took up the leather and began to work. How their needles flew back and forth, back and forth! How their little hammers beat rap-a-tap-tap, rap-a-tap-tap! Almost before the shoemaker and his wife could think, the work was all done. The tiny elves ran about, skipping and dancing. Then, quick as a wink, they were gone.

The next morning the shoemaker said to his wife, "What can we do for those dear little elves?"

"I should like to make some clothes for them," said his wife. "They were almost naked."

"If you will make their coats, I will make them some shoes," said the shoemaker. "Their little feet were bare."

When the clothes and shoes were ready, they were put upon the bench. The shoemaker and his wife again hid behind the curtain. Just as before, when the clock struck twelve, in jumped the tiny elves. They went skipping and dancing to their work. They saw the little coats, the tiny stockings, and the neat little shoes. They clapped their hands for joy. Then, slipping on their clothes, they skipped, hand in hand, out of the window. The shoemaker and his wife never saw the little elves again, but after that night, good luck seemed always to be with them.

Name: _____   Date: _____

"The Shoemaker and the Elves"
from *The Beacon Second Reader*
by James H. Fassett *(cont.)*

Directions: Use the text to answer the questions below.

1 Retell the main events of the story. How do these events relate to the overall message of the text?

_____

_____

_____

_____

2 Explain how the sequence of events and the development of the characters in the text are related. Include specific examples from the text in your answer.

_____

_____

_____

_____

3 What do the man and his wife's actions show you in the last paragraph? Use examples from the text to support your answer.

_____

_____

_____

_____

Excerpt from
Solids
by Lisa Greathouse

Look around you. What do you see? A window? The book you are reading? A chair? It is all **matter**! Matter is the stuff all around us. There are three main kinds of matter: solids, liquids, and gases. Just about everything in the world is one of these.

What Is the Matter?

Which kind of matter do you think this paper is? Well, if it were a liquid, it would be dripping off your desk. If it were a gas, it would be floating away in the air. That must make this paper a solid! A solid is a kind of matter that keeps its own shape. That means that this paper will always look like a book and a chair will always look like a chair. It is hard to change a solid's shape or size. Most solids will not melt if they get hot, and they will not float away.

A solid can be metal, wood, glass, paper, plastic, or cloth. It can be any color. It can be light as a feather or as heavy as a truck. These are called **properties**. Properties are the way an object looks, feels, or acts. Solids are almost always hard because their **particles**, or parts, are packed tightly together. The closer the particles, the harder the solid. For example, a rock has really tight particles!

Solids Can Change

Most of the time, matter stays the same. A solid stays a solid and a liquid stays a liquid. But some matter can change if it gets hot or cold. Can you think of something that can change from a solid to a liquid? How about ice cream left out in the sun? Even when that ice cream melts,

Excerpt from
Solids
by Lisa Greathouse *(cont.)*

it still tastes the same, right? That is because it is still made out of the same particles. When ice cream heats up, its particles get moving. They spread out. That is what makes a solid turn into a liquid.

A solid's properties change when it turns into a liquid. Unlike solids, liquids can change their shape. When you pour water into a tall, skinny glass, the water is tall and skinny. When you pour that same water into a short, wide glass, the water becomes short and wide. That is because a liquid takes on the shape of its container.

Liquids can change, too. When a liquid gets hot, its particles start moving fast. The particles spread out even more and that can make the liquid turn into gas. When you see **steam** coming out of a pot of boiling water, you know that the liquid water is turning into a gas.

Can you think of a kind of matter that you cannot see at all? You are breathing matter right now! The air around you is matter in the form of a gas. The particles in a gas are really spread out and are moving nonstop.

Think of a bowl of noodle soup. It seems like a liquid, right? But the noodles are solids, and it is so hot, there is steam floating out of it. That means there are solids, liquids, and gas in that bowl! That is called a **mixture**.

Name: _____ Date: _____

Excerpt from
Solids
by Lisa Greathouse *(cont.)*

Directions: Use the text to answer the questions below.

1 Summarize the main ideas in the text. Include specific details from the text to support your answer.

_____

_____

_____

_____

2 How does the author elaborate on the idea presented in the first paragraph? Include specific examples from the text to support your answer.

_____

_____

_____

_____

3 Reread the sixth paragraph. How do the ideas in this paragraph relate to the main idea of the text?

_____

_____

_____

_____

Excerpt from
The Jungle Book
by Rudyard Kipling

The Law of the Jungle, which never orders anything without a reason, forbids every beast to eat Man except when he is killing to show his children how to kill, and then he must hunt outside the hunting grounds of his pack or tribe. The real reason for this is that Man killing means, sooner or later, the arrival of white men on elephants, with guns, and hundreds of brown men with gongs and rockets and torches. Then everybody in the jungle suffers. The reason the beasts give among themselves is that Man is the weakest and most defenseless of all living things, and it is unsportsmanlike to touch him. They say too—and it is true—that man-eaters become mangy, and lose their teeth.

The purr grew louder, and ended in the full-throated "Aaarh!" of the tiger's charge.

Then there was a howl—an untigerish howl—from Shere Khan. "He has missed," said Mother Wolf. "What is it?"

Father Wolf ran out a few paces and heard Shere Khan muttering and mumbling savagely as he tumbled about in the scrub.

"The fool has had no more sense than to jump at a woodcutter's campfire, and has burned his feet," said Father Wolf with a grunt.

"Something is coming uphill," said Mother Wolf, twitching one ear. "Get ready."

The bushes rustled a little in the thicket, and Father Wolf dropped with his haunches under him, ready for his leap. Then, if you had been watching, you would have seen the most wonderful thing in the world—the wolf checked in mid-spring. He made his bound before he saw what it was he was jumping at, and then he tried to stop himself. The result was that he shot up straight into the air for four or five feet, landing almost where he left ground.

"Man!" he snapped. "A man's cub. Look!"

Excerpt from

The Jungle Book
by Rudyard Kipling *(cont.)*

Directly in front of him, holding on by a low branch, stood a naked brown baby who could just walk—as soft and as dimpled a little atom as ever came to a wolf's cave at night. He looked up into Father Wolf's face, and laughed.

"Is that a man's cub?" said Mother Wolf. "I have never seen one. Bring it here."

A Wolf accustomed to moving his own cubs can, if necessary, mouth an egg without breaking it, and though Father Wolf's jaws closed right on the child's back not a tooth even scratched the skin as he laid it down among the cubs.

"How little! How naked, and—how bold!" said Mother Wolf softly. The baby was pushing his way between the cubs to get close to the warm hide. "Ahai! He is taking his meal with the others. And so this is a man's cub. Now, was there ever a wolf that could boast of a man's cub among her children?"

Name: _____ Date: _____

Excerpt from
The Jungle Book
by Rudyard Kipling *(cont.)*

Directions: Use the text to answer the questions below.

1 What is the relationship between Father Wolf and Shere Khan? Refer back to the text for specific examples to support your answer.

_____

_____

_____

2 What did you learn about the baby in the paragraph that starts with "Directly in front of him..."? What words did the author use to communicate this information?

_____

_____

_____

3 What is the setting of the text? Include specific words and phrases from the text in your answer.

_____

_____

_____

4 What event comes before the baby's appearance from the brush? Why is this significant?

_____

_____

_____

Collecting Data

Jeremy and Michelle are having a disagreement. Jeremy says that baseball is the most popular sport in their class. Michelle is confident that the most popular sport is football. How can the two friends find the truth?

The first thing that Jeremy and Michelle must do is to get more information. In mathematics, we call this **collecting data**. *Data* means "facts" or "pieces of information." Jeremy and Michelle want to collect data from their classmates. They need to find out which sport is most popular.

How to Collect Data

The first step to gathering data is deciding which method to use. There are many ways to collect data. Here are four of the most common methods.

Observation

To **observe** means to notice. A good example of this is when you keep score in a game. Let us say you want to know how many points each team scores during a volleyball match. The best way to get this data is to watch the match! You can record each point as the teams make it. At the end of the game you will have all the data from that match.

Survey

If you ever watch the news or television game shows, you have probably heard about surveys. A **survey** is a way to collect data. In surveys, you ask many people the same question or questions. Then, you record their answers.

Collecting Data *(cont.)*

Experimentation

Sometimes the information that you need does not already exist or the data is not easy to find. In these cases, you may need to do an **experiment** to gather the data you want. Let us say that you want to know which kind of ball bounces the highest. The best way to gather this data might be to try it out. You could bounce each ball several times and record how high they go. At the end, you could compare the results.

Research

Many times the data you need does exist, but it is not in the form that you need. You need to do **research**. For instance, let us say you wanted to know if taller basketball teams score more points. You would need to compare the average height of the players on each team with their number of wins per season. There are records that show how tall each player is and there are records that show which teams won each game. There may not be a chart that compares the two, however. You could gather the data that you need by researching the information that is already recorded. Then, you could create your own chart and make the comparison.

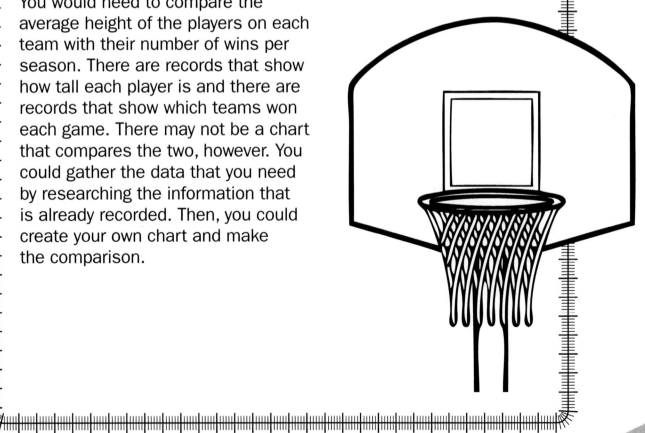

Name: _____   Date: _____

Collecting Data (cont.)

Directions: Use the text to answer the questions below.

1 What are Jeremy and Michelle's role in the text? Why did the author choose to include them? Support your answer with textual evidence.

_____

_____

_____

2 How is the idea of data collection introduced in the text? Include specific examples from the text in your answer.

_____

_____

_____

3 Describe how the information in the paragraphs comes together to contribute to the main topic in the text.

_____

_____

_____

4 What is one problem presented in the text? How is it resolved?

_____

_____

_____

Excerpt from
Call of the Wild
by Jack London

Buck did not read the newspapers or else he would have known that trouble was brewing. Not only for himself, but trouble brewed for every tide-water dog, strong of muscle and with warm, long hair, from Puget Sound to San Diego. Men, groping in the Arctic darkness, had found a yellow metal. Steamship and transportation companies were booming the find and thousands of men were rushing into the Northland. These men wanted heavy dogs with strong muscles by which to toil. They wanted dogs with furry coats to protect them from the frost.

Buck lived at a big house in the sun-kissed Santa Clara Valley. Judge Miller's place, it was called. It stood back from the road, half hidden among the trees, through which glimpses could be caught of the wide cool veranda that ran around its four sides. The house was approached by graveled driveways which wound about through wide-spreading lawns and under the interlacing boughs of tall poplars. At the rear, things were on even a more spacious scale than at the front. There were great stables, where a dozen grooms and boys held forth, rows of vine-clad servants' cottages, an endless and orderly array of outhouses, long grape arbors, green pastures, orchards, and berry patches. Then there was the pumping plant for the artesian well, and the big cement tank where Judge Miller's boys took their morning plunge and kept cool in the hot afternoon.

And over this great demesne Buck ruled. Here he was born, and here he had lived the four years of his life. It was true, there were other dogs. There could not but be other dogs on so vast a place, but they did not count. They came and went. They resided in the populous kennels or lived obscurely in the recesses of the house after the fashion of Toots, the Japanese pug, or Ysabel, the Mexican hairless,—strange creatures that rarely put nose out of doors or set foot to ground. On the other hand, there were the fox terriers who yelped fearful promises at Toots and Ysabel looking out of the windows at them.

But Buck was neither house-dog nor kennel-dog. The whole realm was his. He plunged into the swimming tank or went hunting with the Judge's sons. He escorted Mollie and Alice, the Judge's daughters, on long twilight or early morning rambles. On wintry nights, he lay at the Judge's feet before the roaring library fire. He carried the Judge's grandsons on his back, or rolled them in the grass, and guarded their footsteps through wild adventures down to the fountain in the stable yard, and even beyond, where the paddocks were, and the berry patches. Among the terriers he stalked imperiously, and Toots and Ysabel he utterly ignored, for he was king,—king over all creeping, crawling, flying things of Judge Miller's place, humans included.

Name: _____ Date: _____

Excerpt from
Call of the Wild
by Jack London *(cont.)*

Directions: Use the text to answer the questions below.

1 What words does the author use to describe Buck? What can you infer about Buck from these words?

_____

_____

_____

_____

2 How does Buck act around the other dogs? What do these actions tell you about the relationship between these dogs? Support your answer with details from the text.

_____

_____

_____

_____

3 How does setting affect the life of Buck? How do you know?

_____

_____

_____

_____

4 What is the purpose of the text? Include examples from the text to support your answer.

_____

_____

_____

_____

Excerpt from
Ancient Rome
by Betsey Norris

Imagine living in ancient Rome. You would have definitely been impressed with the largest structure of its day, the Coliseum. It took more than ten years to construct (A.D. 70-82) during the reigns of two Flavian emperors, Vespasian and Titus. It was nicknamed the Flavian Amphitheatre. The Coliseum is 160 feet high (48.8 meters) and has three exterior floors consisting of 80 arches. These arches have provided such strength that this structure has managed to survive thousands of years. This huge building would fit inside two football fields.

The architecture of the Coliseum is a spectacular display of Roman talent and skill. The columns on the first story are Doric. The second floor is Ionic architecture, and Corinthian is used on the third floor.

The Doric column is simple in design. It is very plain, having the least decoration of any of the column types. Without a base, this design is simple, but eloquent.

The Ionic columns are more slender, have bases and are decorated with plain or sculpted frieze. These columns have some curves, but are not as elaborate as the Corinthian columns.

The Corinthian column was more elaborate and ornate than the other Greek column types. The Corinthian column begins with a large, richly molded base and extends down to a shaft that is cylindrical and indented with shallow, vertical channels, or flutings. This column is wider in the middle than at the top or bottom. A Corinthian capital has leaf-like designs and volutes. Friezes above these columns are similar, but smaller than those featured above Ionic columns.

This building actually served a dual purpose at one time. The changers located below the main arena were covered with a wooden floor. During the first 10 years of its existence, the stadium could be filled with water and used for mock naval battles. However, this practice was eventually discontinued. The Romans found that over time the water was damaging the foundation and flooring. After this practice was stopped, the gladiators and the animals were kept below the main arena on this floor as others prepared for the events of the evening.

As an ancient Roman attending an event in the Coliseum, you would be one of 50,000 people entering through one of the 80 ground entrances. You would climb the steps to the top of its four stories. You would look down to view the spectacular sight of all its windows, arches, and columns. The Coliseum had separate entrances for the emperor and the gladiators. The seats in the Coliseum were filled by all, but gender and social class determined the seating arrangement. The women and the poor had the worst seats. They probably stood or sat on hard benches in the fourth tier.

Today, the Coliseum is one of Rome's most famous tourist attractions. Although it is a ruin, it remains one of the best examples of Roman architecture and engineering.

Name: _____ Date: _____

Excerpt from
Ancient Rome
by Betsey Norris *(cont.)*

Directions: Use the text to answer the questions below.

1 How does the author elaborate on the idea presented in the first paragraph of the text? Include specific examples from the text to support your answer.

_____

_____

_____

_____

2 What is the historical significance of the setting of the text? Include examples from the text to support your answer.

_____

_____

_____

_____

3 How is the idea of Roman architecture introduced in the text? Include specific examples from the text in your answer.

_____

_____

_____

_____

4 Compare and contrast the different types of columns in the Coliseum as they are presented in the text.

_____

_____

_____

_____

Excerpt from Chapter 3,
Pride and Prejudice
by Jane Austen

Not all that Mrs. Bennet, however, with the assistance of her five daughters, could ask on the subject, was sufficient to draw from her husband any satisfactory description of Mr. Bingley. They attacked him in various ways—with barefaced questions, ingenious suppositions, and distant surmises; but he eluded the skill of them all, and they were at last obliged to accept the second-hand intelligence of their neighbor, Lady Lucas. Her report was highly favorable. Sir William had been delighted with him. He was quite young, wonderfully handsome, extremely agreeable, and, to crown the whole, he meant to be at the next assembly with a large party. Nothing could be more delightful! To be fond of dancing was a certain step towards falling in love; and very lively hopes of Mr. Bingley's heart were entertained.

"If I can but see one of my daughters happily settled at Netherfield," said Mrs. Bennet to her husband, "and all the others equally well married, I shall have nothing to wish for."

In a few days Mr. Bingley returned Mr. Bennet's visit, and sat about ten minutes with him in his library. He had entertained hopes of being admitted to a sight of the young ladies, of whose beauty he had heard much; but he saw only the father. The ladies were somewhat more fortunate, for they had the advantage of ascertaining from an upper window that he wore a blue coat, and rode a black horse.

An invitation to dinner was soon afterwards dispatched; and already had Mrs. Bennet planned the courses that were to do credit to her housekeeping, when an answer arrived which deferred it all. Mr. Bingley was obliged to be in town the following day, and, consequently, unable to accept the honor of their invitation, etc. Mrs. Bennet was quite disconcerted. She could not imagine what business he could have in town so soon after his arrival in Hertfordshire; and she began to fear that he might be always flying about from one place to another, and never settled at Netherfield as he ought to be. Lady Lucas quieted her fears a little by starting the idea of his being gone to London only to get a large party for the ball; and a report soon followed that Mr. Bingley was to bring twelve ladies and seven gentlemen with him to the assembly. The girls grieved over such a number of ladies, but were comforted the day before the ball by hearing, that instead of twelve he brought only six with him from London—his five sisters and a cousin. And when the party entered the assembly room it consisted of only five altogether—Mr. Bingley, his two sisters, the husband of the eldest, and another young man.

Mr. Bingley was good-looking and gentlemanlike; he had a pleasant countenance, and easy, unaffected manners. His sisters were fine women, with an air of decided fashion. His brother-in-law, Mr. Hurst, merely looked the gentleman; but his friend Mr. Darcy soon drew the attention of the room by his fine, tall person, handsome features, noble mien, and the report which was in general circulation within five minutes after his entrance, of his having ten thousand a year. The gentlemen pronounced him

Excerpt from Chapter 3,
Pride and Prejudice
by Jane Austen (cont.)

to be a fine figure of a man, the ladies declared he was much handsomer than Mr. Bingley, and he was looked at with great admiration for about half the evening, till his manners gave a disgust which turned the tide of his popularity; for he was discovered to be proud; to be above his company, and above being pleased; and not all his large estate in Derbyshire could then save him from having a most forbidding, disagreeable countenance, and being unworthy to be compared with his friend.

Mr. Bingley had soon made himself acquainted with all the principal people in the room; he was lively and unreserved, danced every dance, was angry that the ball closed so early, and talked of giving one himself at Netherfield. Such amiable qualities must speak for themselves. What a contrast between him and his friend! Mr. Darcy danced only once with Mrs. Hurst and once with Miss Bingley, declined being introduced to any other lady, and spent the rest of the evening in walking about the room, speaking occasionally to one of his own party. His character was decided. He was the proudest, most disagreeable man in the world, and everybody hoped that he would never come there again. Amongst the most violent against him was Mrs. Bennet, whose dislike of his general behavior was sharpened into particular resentment by his having slighted one of her daughters.

#51449—TDQs: Strategies for Building Text-Dependent Questions

Name: _____   Date: _____

Excerpt from Chapter 3,
Pride and Prejudice
by Jane Austen *(cont.)*

Directions: Use the text to answer the questions below.

1 How does the time at which the text takes place play a role in the story? Support your answer with examples from the text.

_____

_____

_____

_____

2 What is Mrs. Bennett's motivation in the first paragraph? What words or phrases in the text tell you this?

_____

_____

_____

_____

3 How does Lady Lucas act around Mrs. Bennett and her daughters? What do these actions tell you about the relationship between these individuals? Support your answer with details from the text.

_____

_____

_____

_____

4 Reread the paragraph that starts with "In a few days Mr. Bingley returned..." What is the significance of the event that occurs in this paragraph?

_____

_____

_____

_____

Excerpt from

The Every-Day Life of Abraham Lincoln
by Frances Fisher Browne

Notwithstanding the limitations of every kind which hemmed in the life of young Lincoln, he had an instinctive feeling, born perhaps of his eager ambition, that he should one day attain an exalted position. The first betrayal of this premonition is thus related by Mr. Arnold:

"Lincoln attended court at Booneville, to witness a murder trial, at which one of the Breckenridges from Kentucky made a very eloquent speech for the defense. The boy was carried away with admiration, and was so enthusiastic that, although a perfect stranger, he could not resist expressing his admiration to Breckenridge. He wanted to be a lawyer. He went home, dreamed of courts, and got up mock trials, at which he would defend imaginary prisoners. Several of his companions at this period of his life, as well as those who knew him after he went to Illinois, declare that he was often heard to say, not in joke, but seriously, as if he were deeply impressed rather than elated with the idea: 'I shall someday be President of the United States.' It is stated by many of Lincoln's old friends that he often said while still an obscure man, 'Someday I shall be President.' He undoubtedly had for years some presentiment of this."

At seventeen Lincoln wrote a clear, neat, legible hand, was quick at figures, and able to solve easily any arithmetical problem not going beyond the "Rule of Three." Mr. Arnold, noting these facts, says: "I have in my possession a few pages from his manuscript 'Book of Examples in Arithmetic.' One of these is dated March 1, 1826, and headed 'Discount,' and then follows, in his careful handwriting: 'A definition of Discount,' 'Rules for its computation,' 'Proofs and Various Examples,' worked out in figures, etc.; then 'Interest on money' is treated in the same way, all in his own handwriting. I doubt whether it would be easy to find among scholars of our common or high schools, or any school of boys of the age of seventeen, a better written specimen of this sort of work, or a better knowledge of figures than is indicated by this book of Lincoln's, written at the age of seventeen."

In March, 1828, Lincoln went to work for old Mr. Gentry, the founder of Gentryville. "Early the next month the old gentleman furnished his son Allen with a boat and a cargo of bacon and other produce with which he was to go to New Orleans unless the stock should be sooner disposed of. Abe, having been found faithful and efficient, was employed to accompany the young man. He was paid eight dollars per month, and ate and slept on board." The entire business of the trip was placed in Abraham's hands and this fact tells its own story touching the young man's reputation for capacity and integrity. He had never made the trip, knew nothing of the journey, was unaccustomed to business transactions, had never been much upon the river, but his tact and ability and honesty were so far trusted that the trader was willing to risk the cargo in his care. The delight

Excerpt from
The Every-Day Life of Abraham Lincoln
by Frances Fisher Browne (cont.)

with which the youth swung loose from the shore upon his clumsy craft, with the prospect of a ride of eighteen hundred miles before him, and a vision of the great world of which he had read and thought so much, may be imagined. At this time he had reached the height of six feet and four inches, a length of trunk and limb remarkable even among the tall race of pioneers to which he belonged.

Just before the river expedition, Lincoln had walked with a young girl down to the river to show her his flatboat. She relates a circumstance of the evening which is full of significance. "We were sitting on the banks of the Ohio, or rather on the boat he had made and I said to Abe that the sun was going down. He said to me, 'That's not so; it don't really go down; it seems so. The earth turns from west to east and the revolution of the earth carries us under; we do the sinking, as you call it. The sun, as to us, is comparatively still; the sun's sinking is only an appearance.' I replied, 'Abe, what a fool you are!' I know now that I was the fool, not Lincoln. I am now thoroughly satisfied that he knew the general laws of astronomy and the movements of the heavenly bodies. He was better read then than the world knows or is likely to know exactly. No man could talk to me as he did that night unless he had known something of geography as well as astronomy. He often commented or talked to me about what he had read,— seemed to read it out of the book as he went along. He was the learned boy among us unlearned folks and he took great pains to explain; could do it so simply. He was diffident, too."

Name: _____ Date: _____

Excerpt from
The Every-Day Life of Abraham Lincoln
by Frances Fisher Browne *(cont.)*

Directions: Use the text to answer the questions below.

1 What did you learn about Abraham Lincoln in the fourth paragraph that starts with "In March, 1828, Lincoln went to work..."? What words did the author use to communicate this information?

_____

_____

_____

_____

2 How does setting affect the life of Abraham Lincoln? How do you know?

_____

_____

_____

_____

3 Why does the young girl say, "He was the learned boy among us unlearned folks and he took great pains to explain; could do it so simply..."? How does this dialogue relate to Lincoln's character? Use evidence from the text to support your answer.

_____

_____

_____

_____

4 What is the relationship between the ideas presented in the text and the order in which they are presented?

_____

_____

_____

_____

Language Usage

Text-dependent questions (TDQs) are important to the understanding of language usage. In this section, you will find an overview, sample text-dependent questions/prompts, literary and informational passages, as well as supporting questions/prompts to use with your students. Below is a chart that provides the titles and the recommended grade ranges for the texts in this section.

Grade Range	Literary Text	Page #	Informational Text	Page #
K–1	*Fritz*	128	*Frogs*	130
2–3	*The Three Little Pigs* from *English Fairy Tales* by Anonymous, Collected by Joseph Jacobs	132	*Earth's Layers*	135
4–5	*The Emperor's New Clothes* from *Andersen's Fairy Tales* by Hans Christian Andersen	138	*Being Sick*	141
6–8	Excerpt from Chapter 1, *A Little Princess* by Frances Hodgson Burnett	144	*Irish Immigration*	146
9–12	*The Bravery of Regulus* by Charlotte M. Yonge	148	Excerpt from Chapter 1, *Beethoven* by George Alexander Fischer	151

Language Usage Overview

Text-dependent questions serve as important tools in the exploration, study, and comprehension of the way specific words and phrases convey meaning through text. In order to derive meaning, students must be able to use the context of the words and phrases presented within the text to aid their comprehension. In the English language, words often have multiple meanings and it is only through context that readers can establish the author's intended definition of particular words. For example, the word *cut* can be either a verb or a noun depending on the context. In the case of some words, even the pronunciation differs depending on context. In the sentence, "The many curves on the *windy* road made it very treacherous on that *windy*, wet day" the word *windy* has two different pronunciations as well as definitions. Furthermore, authors use words and phrases in specific ways to create tone, mood, and emotion in their writing. Text-dependent questions teach students how to examine the specific aspects of word choice in order to comprehend the literal meanings of words, as well as the subtleties of the text.

The Common Core State Standards (2010) directly addresses the importance of understanding language usage in Standard 4. This standard mandates that students be able to "interpret words and phrases as they are used in text." The standard explicitly states that students' interpretations of the words and phrases must come directly from the text, reinforcing the need for students to learn to accurately and efficiently reference the text during their learning. Language Anchor Standard 4 goes on to specify that students must be able to determine the "technical, connotative, and figurative meanings" of these words and phrases. In other words, students need to be able to analyze words within the text to understand not only the literal meanings of words, but also the implied meanings. Authors craft their texts to impart specific meanings through word choice. Furthermore, authors frequently employ literary techniques, such as imagery, to add depth and intrigue to their writing. These techniques not only require the reader to understand the meanings of specific words, but also to interpret the comparisons created between the words. Finally, this anchor standard concludes by stating the need for students to be able to "analyze how specific word choices shape meaning or tone." In order to do this, students must synthesize the literal, connotative, and figurative meanings of words in order to grasp how the author's word choice affects the text in a larger sense.

Text-dependent questions allow students to learn how to analyze language usage in a given text at the level of a single word or phrase. These questions can guide students to realize how authors use context to clarify the literal or technical meaning of words. On more complex levels, text-dependent questions also serve to illuminate the role of figurative language in text and teach students about the nuances of language. By employing text-dependent questions as a learning tool in their classrooms, teachers can help their students build an understanding of written language that will enhance comprehension and eventually assist students in their own writing.

Text-Dependent Questions/Prompts

Technical Definitions

- What does the word _____ mean? How does its use in the text support this meaning?

- The word _____ has multiple meanings. Which words in the text helped you figure out the meaning of the word _____?

- What part of speech is the word _____? How can you tell from the context of the sentence?

- What is the meaning of the word _____ as it is used in the _____ paragraph? What are other words the author could have used instead of _____?

- How does the text around the word _____ add to your understanding of the word? Use examples from the text to support your answer.

- Which words in the text show _____? Support your answer with evidence from the text.

- What words does the author use to signal a transition between ideas in the text? How is this helpful for the reader? Support your answer with specific words and phrases from the text.

Connotation

- Why did the author choose to use the word/phrase _____ to describe _____? How did the author's choice of words affect your understanding of the text? Include evidence from the text to support your answer.

- In the _____ paragraph, the author uses the word _____ to make a point to the reader. What does the author want the reader to understand? Use specific words and phrases from the text in your answer.

- What are some synonyms for the word _____ as it is used in the paragraph? Why did the author choose to use _____ instead of a different word?

- What word does the author use to describe _____? How does this word help the reader understand more about _____?

- What are the connotations of the word/phrase _____ as used in the text?

- What does the word/phrase _____ make you think of as it is used in the text?

- Look at the _____ paragraph. What is the difference between the word _____ and the word _____? Why did the author choose to use _____ and not _____ in this text?

- What is implied by the word/phrase _____ as used on page _____ in the text?

- Reread the _____ paragraph. Without looking back at the text, which words do you remember? Why are these words important? Use evidence from the text to support your opinions.

Text-Dependent Questions/Prompts (cont.)

- What if the author used _____ instead of _____? How would that change the story?

- What emotions do the characters experience on page _____ in the text? What words convey/show these emotions? Cite specific words from the text to support your answer.

- Did the author use any words/phrases that surprised you? Cite textual evidence to explain why the author's choice of words was or was not surprising to you.

- Why did the author choose to use the word/phrase _____ on page _____? How did the use of this word affect the reader's understanding of the rest of the sentence/text?

- How would the meaning of the text on page _____ be changed if the author had used the word _____ instead of _____? Include specific evidence from the text to support your answer.

- Reread the _____ paragraph of the story. Why did the author choose to use the word _____? How did this word choice help the reader understand what was going to happen next in the story?

Figurative Language

- Which specific words in the text help the reader visualize _____? Is it effective? Include examples from the text to support your opinion.

- How does the author describe the sights/sounds/smells of _____? Refer back to the text for the specific words and phrases used by the author.

- Which words does the author use to appeal to/to make you use your senses in the _____ paragraph?

- What kind of imagery does the author use in the text/passage/paragraph? Provide specific examples from the text. How does this imagery help the reader comprehend the text?

- What words or phrases could you add to the text to enhance the author's description of _____? How do your suggestions align with the author's existing description?

- What does the author compare to _____ in the text? How does this comparison help the reader understand the text better?

- What is the role of simile/metaphor/personification/etc., in the text? Support your answer with specific information from the text.

- Why did the author choose to compare _____ to _____ in the text? Include specific words and phrases from the text to support your ideas.

- What is the purpose of attributing human characteristics to an inanimate object, such as _____, in the text? Use examples from the text to support your answer.

Text-Dependent Questions/Prompts (cont.)

- Provide an example of alliteration from the text. Why do you think the author chose to play with language in this way? What effect does the alliteration create?

- What is the difference between a simile and a metaphor? Why did the author choose to use a _____ and not a _____ in this text?

- Is the comparison between _____ and _____ effective? Why or why not? Refer back to the text for specific examples to support your opinion.

- How does the author's use of hyperbole enhance the description of _____ in the text? Use specific words and phrases from the text to illustrate your answer.

- What type of figurative language does the author use to describe _____? Be sure to include specific examples from the text in your answer.

- How does the author's use of figurative language in the text affect the way the reader views _____ in the story? Support your answer with examples from the text.

Tone

- What emotions do you feel as you read the text? What words does the author use to create a sense of emotion for the reader?

- What is the tone of the text? What language does the author use to create this tone? Cite specific examples from the text.

- How does the word/phrase _____ support the tone of the text? Use examples from the text in your answer.

- Does the author use a formal or casual tone in the text? What specific words or phrases in the text support this?

- How does the characters' dialogue contribute to the tone of the text? Be sure to reference examples of dialogue in your answer.

- How do the characters' actions affect the tone of the text? Provide examples from the text to support your answer.

- Does the text have a generally negative or positive tone? How do specific word choices contribute to the overall tone?

- How does the tone of the text affect the reader's perception of the information conveyed in the writing? Explicitly reference the text in your answer.

- How do you think the author feels about the subject matter presented in the text? What clues in the language of the text convey the author's attitude?

- What is the author's attitude toward/How do you think the author feels about _____? What specific words in the text make you think this?

- What language/words does the author use to signify a shift in the tone of the text in paragraph/sentence _____?

Text-Dependent Questions/Prompts *(cont.)*

- What words does the author use to tell you about the genre of the story? Why is it helpful for the reader to understand the genre? Use specific words or phrases from the text to support your answer.

- What is the relationship between the use of imagery and the tone of the text? Cite textual evidence to support your answer.

- What do you imagine the author's personality to be like? How is this personality expressed through the language in the text? Use specific examples from the text to explain your thinking.

- Do you think the author knows a lot about _____? What about the text makes you feel this way?

Fritz

Fritz is a very playful dog.

He loves to play fetch.

Jen throws the ball for Fritz.

Fritz brings it back to Jen.

Fritz also likes to go for walks.

Jen takes him to the park every day.

He loves to play with the other dogs.

The dogs chase each other.

They also roll in the grass.

#51449—TDQs: Strategies for Building Text-Dependent Questions

Name: _____ Date: _____

Fritz (cont.)

Directions: Use the text to answer the questions below.

1 What does the word *playful* mean?
How do you know?

_____

- - - - - - - - - - - - - - - - - -

_____
_____

- - - - - - - - - - - - - - - - - -

_____
_____

- - - - - - - - - - - - - - - - - -

_____

2 What if the author used the word *old* instead of
playful? How would that change the story?

_____

- - - - - - - - - - - - - - - - - -

_____
_____

- - - - - - - - - - - - - - - - - -

_____
_____

- - - - - - - - - - - - - - - - - -

_____

Frogs

Frogs lay their eggs in the water. Tadpoles hatch from the eggs.

They grow arms and legs as they get bigger. Their tails disappear. Then, they become frogs.

Frogs take in water through their skin. They must live near water. Their skin will dry out if they don't.

Frogs eat mostly bugs. They catch the bugs with their sticky tongues.

Frogs have amazing eyes. Their eyes can see in many directions at the same time. Frogs never close their eyes. They even sleep with them open!

Name: _____   Date: _____

Frogs <small>(cont.)</small>

Directions: Use the text to answer the questions below.

1 Why did the author choose to use the word *amazing* to describe a frog's eyes? What words in the text make you think this?

_____

— — — — — — — — — — — — — — — — — —

_____

_____

— — — — — — — — — — — — — — — — — —

_____

_____

— — — — — — — — — — — — — — — — — —

_____

2 What word does the author use to describe the frog's tongue? How does this word help you understand more about a frog?

_____

— — — — — — — — — — — — — — — — — —

_____

_____

— — — — — — — — — — — — — — — — — —

_____

_____

— — — — — — — — — — — — — — — — — —

_____

The Three Little Pigs

from *English Fairy Tales*
by Anonymous, Collected by Joseph Jacobs

Once upon a time there were three little pigs. Each pig wanted to build a house for himself. The first little pig met a man carrying straw. "Please give me that straw so I can build a house" said the little pig. The man gave the straw to the pig and the little pig built a house with it. Then along came a wolf. The wolf knocked at the door, and said, "Little pig, little pig, let me come in." The pig answered, "No, not by the hair of my chinny chin chin." "Then I'll huff and I'll puff, and I'll blow your house in!" said the Wolf. So he huffed and he puffed, and he blew in the house.

The second pig met a man with a bundle of wood. He said, "Please give me that wood to build a house." The man gave him the wood and the pig built his house. Then along came the wolf. He said, "Little pig, little pig, let me come in." The second pig answered "No, not by the hair of my chinny chin chin." "Then I'll puff and I'll huff, and I'll blow your house in!" cried the wolf. So he huffed and he puffed, and he puffed and he huffed. And at last he blew the house down.

The third little pig met a man with a load of bricks, and said, "Please, give me those bricks so I can build my house." The man gave him the bricks, and he built his house with them.

#51449—TDQs: Strategies for Building Text-Dependent Questions

The Three Little Pigs

from *English Fairy Tales*
by Anonymous, Collected by Joseph Jacobs *(cont.)*

So the wolf came, as he did to the other little pigs, and said, "Little pig, little pig, let me come in."

"No, no, by the hair of my chinny chin chin," replied the third pig. "Then I'll huff and I'll puff, and I'll blow your house in." The wolf huffed and he puffed, and he huffed and he puffed. But he could not blow the house down.

Now the wolf was very angry. He told the third little pig that he would come down the chimney and eat him up. When the little pig heard this, he built a blazing fire. He hung a pot full of water over it. Just as the wolf jumped down the chimney, the little pig pulled the cover off the pot. The wolf fell in the pot. The wolf yowled in pain and leapt out of the pot. He ran out of the house as fast as he could. The wolf never bothered the little pigs again.

Name: _____   Date: _____

The Three Little Pigs
from *English Fairy Tales*
by Anonymous, Collected by Joseph Jacobs *(cont.)*

Directions: Use the text to answer the questions below.

1 What words does the author use to tell you about the genre of the story? Why is it helpful for the reader to understand the genre? Use specific words or phrases from the text to support your answer.

_____

_____

_____

_____

2 Reread the last paragraph of the story. Why did the author choose to use the word *blazing*? How did this word choice help you understand what was going to happen next in the story?

_____

_____

_____

_____

3 Which words does the author use to make you use your senses in the last paragraph?

_____

_____

#51449—TDQs: Strategies for Building Text-Dependent Questions   © Shell Education

Earth's Layers

Did you know that Earth has many layers? It may seem like Earth is one big rock, but that is not the case. Earth actually has four main layers.

The outer layer is called the crust. People live on Earth's **crust**. Earth's crust is made of huge sections called plates. Even though our ground seems very stable, it is actually floating. The plates of Earth's crust float on the next layer. That layer is called the mantle. These plates move very slowly, but they are always in motion. The place where two plates come together is called a **fault**. When two plates rub against each other, they cause an earthquake. When two plates bump into each other, they push the ground upwards and make new mountains. Sometimes, one plate slides under another plate and this makes a trench, or deep, narrow hole, in Earth's crust.

Underneath the crust is Earth's **mantle**. This layer is much thicker than the crust. The heat from Earth's core causes rocks in the mantle to rise towards the crust. As the rocks rise, they start to cool and fall back towards the core. When the mantle breaks through the crust, a volcano is formed. Volcanoes spew hot rocks and molten lava from Earth's mantle. After an eruption, the rocks and lava cool and become part of Earth's crust.

Earth's Layers (cont.)

The inside of Earth is called the **core**. There is an inner core and outer core. The outer core is underneath the mantle. This layer is made up of the metals iron and nickel. The outer core is very, very hot. This heat causes the iron and nickel to melt and become liquids.

The innermost layer of Earth is the **inner core**. The inner core is also made up of iron and nickel. The inner core is under great pressure because it is very deep inside Earth. This pressure causes the iron and nickel to be solids. The inner core is the hottest place on Earth. It is about the same temperature as the surface of the sun!

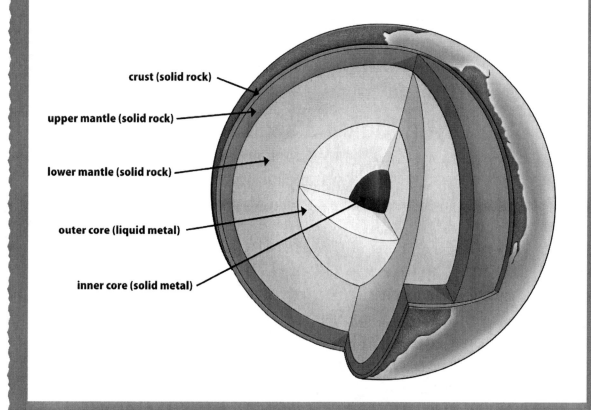

crust (solid rock)

upper mantle (solid rock)

lower mantle (solid rock)

outer core (liquid metal)

inner core (solid metal)

#51449—TDQs: Strategies for Building Text-Dependent Questions

Name: _____ Date: _____

Earth's Layers (cont.)

Directions: Use the text to answer the questions below.

1 The word *plates* has multiple meanings. Which words helped you figure out the meaning of the word *plates* in this text?

_____

_____

_____

2 Why did the author choose the word *spew* to describe a volcanic eruption? How did the author's choice of words affect your understanding of the text? Be sure to include evidence from the text to support your answer.

_____

_____

_____

_____

3 In the second paragraph, the author uses the word *actually* to make a point. What does the author want the reader to understand? Use specific words and phrases from the text in your answer.

_____

_____

_____

_____

The Emperor's New Clothes
from *Andersen's Fairy Tales*
by Hans Christian Andersen

Once upon a time, there lived an Emperor who loved new clothes. He loved clothes so much, he spent all of his money buying them. The only reason he ever went out of the castle was to show off his new clothes. He had a different suit for each hour of the day.

One day, two men arrived at the Emperor's court. They had a plan to fool the Emperor. The men claimed they could weave the most beautiful cloth in the world. They also said that clothes made from their cloth were magical because only wise people were able to see the clothes. Foolish people could not see them.

The Emperor was delighted. He asked the men to make him a new suit with the magical cloth. The men agreed to weave the cloth and make the suit. The Emperor gave them lots of gold and told them to start working. Then he began to plan a parade to show off his new clothes. Soon the whole town was excited about the Emperor's new magical suit of clothes.

So the men set up two looms and pretended to start working. They asked for gold thread and expensive silk. When the Emperor's men brought them, the two scoundrels put the supplies in their bags. Then they pretended to work until late at night at their looms.

The Emperor was excited. He wanted to see his new clothes. The Emperor sent an officer to check on the weavers. When the officer entered the room, he could not see any magical thread or cloth. He was very upset. Then he remembered that only wise men could see the cloth. The officer did not want to appear foolish in front of the Emperor. He lied and told the Emperor that he had seen a magnificent cloth. The officer said the cloth had colors more beautiful than a rainbow. He said he had never seen more intricate patterns. The Emperor could hardly wait to see his new suit.

The Emperor's New Clothes
from *Andersen's Fairy Tales*
by Hans Christian Andersen *(cont.)*

Finally the weavers announced that the suit was finished. The Emperor and his men went to see the suit. When they entered the room, no one could see the magical clothing. Neither the Emperor nor his men wanted to admit that they couldn't see the clothing. They did not want to seem foolish or unworthy. Everyone praised the imaginary clothes and pretended to see them.

The two men asked the Emperor to undress. They pretended to dress him in the imaginary suit. The Emperor's men praised his new clothes. They told him he looked magnificent. The Emperor pretended to admire the new clothes. No one wanted to look like a fool for not being able to see the clothing.

The Emperor went outside to lead the parade. He was only wearing his underwear! All of the townspeople were shocked. They did not say anything though. They did not want to appear foolish because they could not see the magical clothing. Everyone clapped and cheered.

Finally a child said, "The Emperor is only wearing his underwear!" Everyone gasped. Now everyone knew it was true. The Emperor turned red. He was embarrassed because he knew it was true too. He would not admit it though. He continued to march through the town in his underwear. Eventually he reached his castle. The parade ended and the Emperor went inside and put on some real clothes.

Name: _____   Date: _____

The Emperor's New Clothes
from *Andersen's Fairy Tales*
by Hans Christian Andersen *(cont.)*

Directions: Use the text to answer the questions below.

1 Reread the second paragraph. Why did the author choose to use the word *claimed* and not the word *said* in this particular text?

_____

_____

_____

2 Reread the fourth paragraph. What is the meaning of the word *scoundrel* as it is used in this paragraph? Provide evidence from the text to support your answer.

_____

_____

_____

3 What does the officer compare the colors in the imaginary cloth to? How does this comparison help you understand the text better?

_____

_____

_____

4 What do you imagine the author's personality to be like? How is this personality expressed through the language in the text? Use specific examples from the text to explain your thinking.

_____

_____

_____

Being Sick

No one enjoys being sick. When you are sick, your body hurts. You might have a runny nose, a fever, an itchy rash, or a headache. Sometimes, you have multiple symptoms. Being sick means you usually have to stay home from school or work. You cannot play sports, see friends, or go out to stores or restaurants. Being sick is no fun.

Everyone gets sick sometimes, but there are many things you can do to help prevent yourself from getting sick. One important thing you can do is practice good personal hygiene. This means taking care of your body. It is important to bathe regularly to keep your skin and hair healthy. Brushing and flossing are also important. When we eat, food particles build up in our mouths and gums. These particles cause bacteria to build up and these bacteria can lead to cavities and gum disease. Washing your hands is another ideal way to help keep yourself healthy. Hand washing helps prevent bacteria and viruses which cause illness. It is especially important to wash your hands before preparing or eating food. You should also wash your hands after going to the bathroom, coughing or sneezing, or handling garbage. Finally, make sure to get enough sleep. Sleep allows your body to be well-rested so it can fight off sickness.

You can also prevent illness by making healthy food choices. Make sure to eat a variety of different foods. Fruits and vegetables contain important vitamins and minerals for your body. Lean meats, like chicken and fish, give your body protein. Protein can help your body battle infections. Nuts, seeds, and beans are also good sources of protein. Milk and dairy products contain protein as well as calcium for strong bones. It is also important to limit unhealthy foods. Foods that contain a lot of sugar, fat, and salt are not good for your body. These foods can weaken your body if you eat them regularly. When your body is weak, it is easier to get sick.

Being Sick (cont.)

Finally, it is important to see your doctor regularly. At your check-up, your doctor will make sure you are healthy. They measure your height and weight. They check to make sure you are growing. Your doctor will check your eyes and ears to make sure you can see and hear well. Doctors also check the body for signs of illness. At your visit to your doctor, you may get an immunization. Immunizations can prevent serious illnesses like measles and polio. These diseases can make your body very sick. Immunizations can help your body ward off the viruses that cause them.

Getting sick occasionally is part of life. Everyone gets a cold or cough sometimes. However, you can help protect your body from illness. Good personal hygiene, healthy eating habits, and regular visits to the doctor can all help you stay healthy.

#51449—TDQs: Strategies for Building Text-Dependent Questions

Name: _____ Date: _____

Being Sick (cont.)

Directions: Use the text to answer the questions below.

1 How does the text around the word *hygiene* add to your understanding of the word? Use examples from the text to support your answer.

_____

_____

_____

2 Reread the second paragraph. Without looking back at the text, which words do you remember? Why are these words important? Use evidence from the text to support your opinions.

_____

_____

_____

3 What type of figurative language does the author use to describe how the body deals with illness? Include specific examples from the text in your answer.

_____

_____

_____

4 What is the tone of the text? What language does the author use to create this tone? Cite specific examples from the text.

_____

_____

_____

Excerpt from Chapter 1,

A Little Princess

by Frances Hodgson Burnett

On a dark winter's day, when a yellow fog hung thick and heavy in the streets of London, an odd-looking little girl sat in a cab with her father. She sat with her feet tucked under her, and leaned against her father, who held her in his arm. The little girl stared out of the window at the passing people with a queer old-fashioned thoughtfulness in her big eyes.

She was such a little girl that one did not expect to see such a look on her small face. It would have been an old look for a child of twelve, and Sara Crewe was only seven. The fact was, however, that she was always dreaming and thinking odd things. She felt as if she had lived a long, long time.

At this moment she was remembering the voyage she had just made from Bombay with her father, Captain Crewe. She was thinking of the big ship, of the sailors passing silently to and fro on it, of the children playing about on the hot deck, and of some young officers' wives who used to try to make her talk to them and laugh at the things she said. Principally, she was thinking of what a strange thing it was that at one time one was in India in the blazing sun, and then in the middle of the ocean, and then driving in a strange vehicle through strange streets where the day was as dark as the night. She found this so puzzling that she moved closer to her father.

"Papa," she said in a low, mysterious little voice that was almost a whisper, "Papa."

"What is it, darling?" Captain Crewe answered, holding her closer and looking down into her face. "What is Sara thinking of?"

"Is this the place?" Sara whispered, cuddling still closer to him. "Is it, Papa?"

"Yes, little Sara, it is. We have reached it at last." And though she was only seven years old, she knew that he felt sad when he said it.

It seemed to her many years since he had begun to prepare her for "the place," as she always called it. Her mother had died when she was born, so she had never known or missed her. Her young, handsome, rich, petting father seemed to be the only relation she had in the world. She only knew he was rich because she had heard people say so when they thought she was not listening, and she had also heard them say that when she grew up she would be rich, too. That, however, was all she knew about it.

During her short life only one thing had troubled her, and that thing was "the place" she was to be taken to someday. The climate of India was very bad for children, and as soon as possible they were sent away from it—generally to England and to school. She had seen other children go away, and had heard their fathers and mothers talk about the letters they received from them. She had known that she would be obliged to go also, and though sometimes her father's stories of the voyage and the new country had attracted her, she had been troubled by the thought that he could not stay with her for as long as she could remember.

Name: _____ Date: _____

Excerpt from Chapter 1,
A Little Princess
by Frances Hodgson Burnett *(cont.)*

Directions: Use the text to answer the questions below.

1 Reread the first paragraph. Without looking back at the text, which words do you remember? Why are these words important? Use evidence from the text to support your opinions.

_____

_____

_____

_____

2 What does the word *relation* mean? How does its use in the text support this meaning?

_____

_____

_____

_____

3 What kind of imagery does the author use in the passage? Provide specific examples from the text. How does this imagery help the reader comprehend the text?

_____

_____

_____

_____

4 What is the tone of the passage? How does the author use particular words and phrases to create this tone?

_____

_____

_____

_____

Irish Immigration

During the 1800s, many Irish peasants were farmers that lived in poverty. They grew potatoes on small pieces of land and that was their main source of food. In 1845, all of the farmers' potatoes began to rot. No one understood why the potatoes were dying. We know now that a potato fungus was killing the potatoes, but no one knew that at the time.

The Great Potato Famine lasted for five years. Many, many people died of starvation.

As the famine spread, more and more Irish left Ireland. Some went to Great Britain and Canada. Many Irish immigrants came to the United States. These immigrants traveled to America in crowded ships. The living conditions onboard were awful. So many people died on these ships that they became known as "coffin ships."

Irish immigrants faced harsh conditions once they arrived in America, too. Most immigrants had very little money. As a result, they had to settle in the port cities in which they arrived because they could not afford to keep traveling. Many Irish immigrants settled in the port cities of Boston, Philadelphia, and New York. These immigrants lived in crowded basements and tenement buildings. Unsanitary living conditions caused disease to spread quickly in these areas.

Irish immigrants took many different kinds of jobs in America. Irish men often went into labor work. They dug canals, laid rails, and worked in construction. They also became police officers and firefighters. Women immigrants often became maids or worked in the mills. Some went on to become teachers and nurses. Regardless of the type of job, Irish immigrants faced high levels of discrimination in the workplace. Employers often stated that "No Irish Need Apply" in job listings and immigrants were given only the lowest, most undesirable jobs.

The discrimination and prejudice suffered by Irish immigrants caused them to turn to each other for support. They formed strong Irish communities in the cities where they lived. These communities allowed them to carry on Irish traditions and helped them survive. The Irish Catholic Church played a central role in these communities. These churches served as gathering places as well as religious institutions. Religion was an important part of life in Ireland and continued to be for immigrants in America.

Over time, the discrimination against the Irish began to decrease. The children of Irish immigrants gained access to better education and more skilled jobs. As more immigrants continued to arrive from other parts of Europe, the Irish no longer had to take the most undesirable jobs. Instead, they became bosses and foremen as these new immigrants filled the need for unskilled laborers.

Today, many Americans proudly celebrate their Irish heritage. For example, the Irish holiday, St. Patrick's Day, is celebrated across the country. Irish Americans no longer face discrimination in the workplace. Many have finally achieved the lifestyles and opportunities their immigrant ancestors sought long ago.

Name: _____ Date: _____

Irish Immigration (cont.)

Directions: Use the text to answer the questions below.

1 What is the meaning of the word *unsanitary* as it is used in the fourth paragraph? What are other words the author could have used instead of *unsanitary*?

_____

_____

_____

_____

2 Why did the author say that the ships were known as "coffin ships"? How does this use of language help the reader comprehend the text on a deeper level?

_____

_____

_____

_____

3 What is the tone at the beginning of the text? Does the tone of the text remain the same throughout? Support your answer with evidence from the text.

_____

_____

_____

_____

4 How do you think the author feels about the subject matter presented in the text? What clues in the language of the text convey the author's attitude?

_____

_____

_____

_____

The Bravery of Regulus
by Charlotte M. Yonge

The first wars that the Romans engaged in beyond the bounds of Italy were with the Carthaginians. The initial dispute between Rome and Carthage was about their possession of the island of Sicily; and the war thus begun had lasted eight years, when Rome resolved to send an army to fight the Carthaginians on their own shores. The army and fleet were placed under the command of the two consuls, Lucius Manlius and Marcus Attilius Regulus. On the way, there was a great sea-fight with the Carthaginian fleet, and this was the first naval battle that the Romans ever won. It made the way to Africa free, but the soldiers, who had never been so far from home before, murmured, for they expected to meet not only human enemies, but monstrous serpents, lions, elephants, and dog-headed monsters. They imagined a scorching sun overhead and a noisome marsh under their feet. Regulus sternly put a stop to all murmurs by making it known that disaffection would be punished by death, and the army safely landed, and set up a fortification at Clypea, and plundered the whole country round. Then orders came from Rome that Manlius should return thither, but that Regulus should remain to carry on the war.

The country was most beautiful, covered with fertile corn-fields and full of rich fruit trees. All the rich Carthaginians had country-houses and gardens, which were made delicious with fountains, trees, and flowers. The Roman soldiers, plain, hardy, fierce, and pitiless, did, it must be feared, cruel damage among these peaceful scenes. They boasted of having sacked 300 villages, and mercy was not yet known to them. The Carthaginian army, though strong in horsemen and in elephants, kept upon the hills and did nothing to save the country, and the wild desert tribes of Numidians came rushing in to plunder what the Romans had left. The Carthaginians sent to offer terms of peace, but Regulus, who had become uplifted by his conquests, made such demands that the messengers remonstrated. He answered, "Men who are good for anything should either conquer or submit to their betters;" and he sent them rudely away. Regulus's merit was that he had no more mercy on himself than on others.

The Carthaginians were driven to extremity. They had sent, in their distress, to hire soldiers in Greece, and among these came a Spartan, named Xanthippus, who at once took the command and led the army out to battle, with a long line of elephants ranged in front of them, and with clouds of horsemen hovering on the wings. The Romans had not yet learned the best mode of fighting with elephants, namely, to leave lanes in their columns where these huge beasts might advance harmlessly. Instead, the ranks were thrust and trampled down by the creatures' bulk and they suffered a terrible defeat. Regulus himself was seized by the horsemen, and dragged into Carthage, where the victors feasted and rejoiced through half the night. They testified their thanks to the gods by offering the bravest of their captives to their fires.

Regulus himself was not, however, one of these victims. He was kept a close prisoner for two years and at last a victory so decisive was gained by the Romans, that the people of Carthage were discouraged, and resolved to ask terms of peace.

The Bravery of Regulus
by Charlotte M. Yonge (cont.)

They thought that no one would be so readily listened to in Rome as Regulus, and they therefore sent him there with their envoys, having first made him swear that he would come back to his prison if there should neither be peace nor an exchange of prisoners. They little knew how much more a true-hearted Roman cared for his city than for himself and for his word than for his life.

Worn and dejected, the captive warrior came to the outside of the gates of his own city, and there paused, refusing to enter. "I am no longer a Roman citizen," he said, "I am but the barbarians' slave, and the Senate may not give audience to strangers within the walls." His wife Marcia ran out to greet him, with his two sons, but he did not look up, and instead received their caresses as one beneath their notice, as a mere slave.

The Roman Senate, as he would not come in to them, came out to hold their meeting in the Campagna. The ambassadors spoke first, then Regulus, standing up, said, as one repeating a task, "Conscript fathers, being a slave to the Carthaginians, I come on the part of my masters to treat with you concerning peace, and an exchange of prisoners." He then turned to go away with the ambassadors, as a stranger might not be present at the deliberations of the Senate. His old friends pressed him to stay and finally, at the command of his Carthaginian masters, he remained, though not taking his seat.

He told the Roman senators to persevere in the war. He said he had seen the distress of Carthage, and that a peace would be only to her advantage, not to that of Rome, and therefore he strongly advised that the war should continue. Then, as to the exchange of prisoners, he reported that the Carthaginian generals, who were in the hands of the Romans, were in full health and strength, whilst he himself was too much broken down to be fit for service again. Thus he insisted that no exchange of prisoners should be made.

It was wonderful, even to Romans, to hear a man thus pleading against himself, and their chief priest came forward, and declared that, as his oath had been wrested from him by force, he was not bound by it to return to his captivity. But Regulus was too noble to listen to this for a moment. "Have you resolved to dishonor me?" he said. "I am not ignorant that death and the more extreme tortures await me, but what are these to the shame of an infamous action, or the wounds of a guilty mind? Slave as I am to Carthage, I have still the spirit of a Roman. I have sworn to return. It is my duty to go; let the gods take care of the rest."

The Senate decided to follow the advice of Regulus, though they bitterly regretted his sacrifice. His wife wept and entreated in vain that they would detain him. They could merely repeat their permission to him to remain, but nothing could prevail with him to break his word, and he turned back to the chains and death he expected as calmly as if he had been returning to his home. This was in the year B.C. 249.

Name: _____ Date: _____

The Bravery of Regulus
by Charlotte M. Yonge (cont.)

Directions: Use the text to answer the questions below.

1 What is the author's attitude toward Regulus? What specific words in the text make you think this?

_____

_____

_____

_____

2 Which specific words in the text help the reader visualize Carthage? Is it effective? Include examples from the text to support your opinion.

_____

_____

_____

_____

3 The word *extremity* has multiple meanings. Which words helped you figure out the meaning of the word *extremity* in this text?

_____

_____

_____

_____

4 How does the language of this text relate to its genre? Why is this information helpful for the reader? Include specific examples from the text in your answer.

_____

_____

_____

_____

Excerpt from Chapter 1,

Beethoven

by *George Alexander Fischer*

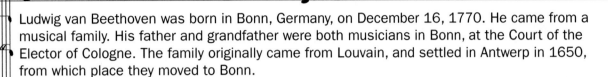

Ludwig van Beethoven was born in Bonn, Germany, on December 16, 1770. He came from a musical family. His father and grandfather were both musicians in Bonn, at the Court of the Elector of Cologne. The family originally came from Louvain, and settled in Antwerp in 1650, from which place they moved to Bonn.

This old city on the Rhine, the scene of innumerable battles from Roman times up to the beginning of the nineteenth century, has much that is interesting about it, but is distinguished chiefly on account of having been Beethoven's birthplace. It was for five centuries (from 1268 to 1794) in the possession of the Electors of Cologne. The last one of all, Max Franz, who succeeded to the Electorate when Beethoven was fourteen years of age, was a highly cultivated person, especially in music. He was the youngest son of Maria Therese, Empress of Austria, herself a fine singer and well versed in the music of the time. The Elector played the viola and his chief interest in life seems to have been music. In Beethoven's time and long before, the aristocracy led lives of easy, complacent enjoyment, dabbling in art, patronizing music and the composers, seemingly with no prevision that the musicians whom they attached to their train, and who in the cases of Mozart and Haydn were at times treated but little better than lackeys, were destined by the irony of fate to occupy places in the temple of fame, which would be denied themselves.

Ludwig van Beethoven, the grandfather of the composer, received his appointment as Kapellmeister, or leader of the orchestra, at Bonn in March of 1733, then twenty-one years of age. The grandfather was in every way a worthy man, but he died when our composer was three years of age, and from that time poverty and hardship of all kinds afflicted the family. Beethoven's father was careless and improvident. His salary of 300 florins, about $145, was all they had upon which to live. The mother was the daughter of a cook. She was kind-hearted, of pleasant temper and lovable disposition, and the affection between mother and son was deep and lasting. The father was stern, and a strict disciplinarian. He was determined that the son should do better than himself, being willing to furnish the precept, if not the example.

Reared in this school of adversity, the boy had a hard life. His father was his first teacher, teaching him both violin and clavier. Before he was nine years of age, however, the boy's progress was so great that the father had no more to teach him.

In those times the musical life centered about the Court. Beethoven studied the organ under the court organist, Christian Neefe, starting at eleven years of age and Neefe had an important bearing on Beethoven's life. He was in his best years, thirty-three, when he began teaching him, and was a thorough musician and a university man as well. Neefe saw the boy's talent and became his friend. On one occasion the Elector took his musicians to Münster and left Beethoven, then under twelve years of age, behind as the organist.

After the Münster episode, the twelve-year-old Beethoven became the regular substitute. When we consider the important role that church music played in those times, such precocity is remarkable. This connection with church music bore good fruit in later years.

Excerpt from Chapter 1,
Beethoven
by George Alexander Fischer *(cont.)*

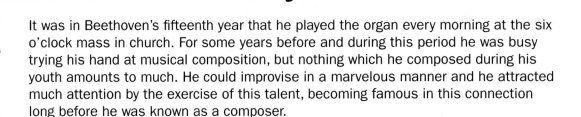

It was in Beethoven's fifteenth year that he played the organ every morning at the six o'clock mass in church. For some years before and during this period he was busy trying his hand at musical composition, but nothing which he composed during his youth amounts to much. He could improvise in a marvelous manner and he attracted much attention by the exercise of this talent, becoming famous in this connection long before he was known as a composer.

His creative talent unfolded itself slowly. He had high ideals and worked faithfully toward their attainment. Failure to reach the level of his aspirations did not dishearten him; rather it spurred him on to greater effort.

The discerning intellect is always in advance of the creative. His delight in Bach was great; he studied him to such purpose that, at twelve years, he was able to play the greater part of the Well-tempered Clavichord. His wonderful interpretation of Bach, later, on his arrival in Vienna, immediately placed him in the front rank of virtuosi.

As a boy he was docile, shy and reserved, caring nothing for the ordinary games of boys, or at least not participating in them to any extent. At an age when other boys begin learning their games, he began in composition, being forced to it, no doubt, by his father. He is said to have written a cantata at the age of ten to the memory of an English friend of the family, who died early in the year 1781.

From year to year he kept on in musical composition, feeling his way, not discouraged by his inability to produce anything great, although Mozart's precocity and genius were no doubt frequently held up to him by others as an example to profit by. When he was seventeen he went to Vienna. There he met Mozart, then at the height of his fame, whose operas were frequently produced in Bonn and throughout Germany. He probably had some lessons from him. As Beethoven's visit terminated in three months, it is not likely that he derived much benefit from these lessons, but the fact that this was a momentous occasion to the impressionable Beethoven is certain. The emotions called up by the presence of Mozart enabled him to play with such effect that when he had finished, Mozart made the well-known remark: "Pay attention to him. He will make a noise in the world someday."

Beethoven, however, was compelled to return to Bonn, owing to the serious illness of his mother, who died of consumption July 17, 1787. He now took charge of the family and had a hard life from almost every point of view, his one enjoyment probably being in the exercise of his art. The affection between mother and son was one of the few bright spots in a boyhood of toil and privation. Beethoven felt her death keenly and was thrust into adulthood without the benefits of her love and support.

#51449—TDQs: Strategies for Building Text-Dependent Questions

Name: _____   Date: _____

Excerpt from Chapter 1,
Beethoven
by *George Alexander Fischer* (cont.)

Directions: Use the text to answer the questions below.

1 What are the connotations of the word *dabbling* in the second paragraph? Use specific words and phrases from the text to support your answer.

_____

_____

_____

_____

2 Reread the second to last paragraph. What is the meaning of the word *precocity*? How do you know?

_____

_____

_____

_____

3 How does the phrase, "Reared in the school of adversity" support the tone of the text? Use examples from the text in your answer.

_____

_____

_____

_____

4 What type of figurative language does the author use to describe the importance of Beethoven's first experience as a church organist? Include specific examples from the text.

_____

_____

_____

_____

#51449—TDQs: Strategies for Building Text-Dependent Questions

© Shell Education

Text Structure

Text-dependent questions (TDQs) are important to the understanding of text structure. In this section, you will find an overview, sample text-dependent questions/prompts, literary and informational passages, as well as supporting questions/prompts to use with your students. Below is a chart that provides the titles and the recommended grade ranges for the texts in this section.

Grade Range	Literary Text	Page #	Informational Text	Page #
K–1	*My Pets*	163	*Whales*	165
2–3	Excerpt from *Peter Rabbit* by Beatrix Potter	167	*Understanding Place Value*	170
4–5	Excerpt from *The Celebrated Jumping Frog of Calaveras County* by Mark Twain	172	*Early American Indians in the Southwestern United States*	175
6–8	Excerpt from *Macbeth* by William Shakespeare, Act I, Scene VII	178	*Our Wondrous Solar System*	180
9–12	*Excerpt from Crime and Punishment, Part I, Chapter I* by Fyodor Dostoevsky	182	Excerpt from *The Byzantine Empire: A Society that Shaped the World* by Kelly Rodgers	185

Text Structure Overview

When learning to analyze and comprehend text, students often gravitate towards the content of the text and fail to consider the more subtle aspects of text structure. Text-dependent questions are an effective way to guide students to see the ways in which the text structure affects the overall content and message. In the same way that text-dependent questions can be used to help the reader identify both the literal and connotative meanings of specific word choices, these questions can also enable students to see how sentences, paragraphs, and organizational structures interact to convey meaning. According to Fisher, Frey, and Alfaro (2013), text-dependent questions about vocabulary and text structure allow students to "bridge literal and inferential meanings" through the examination of "word choice, connotations, and organizational structure" (128). By understanding the role of structure, students learn how to analyze and examine various aspects of a text, such as theme, emotion, tone, central ideas, and meaning.

The importance of text structure is clearly highlighted in the Common Core State Standards (2010). Reading Anchor Standard 5 requires students to be able to, "analyze the structure of texts, including how specific sentences, paragraphs, and larger portions of the text relate to each other and the whole." The Common Core Standards then break this anchor standard down into grade-specific standards for both literature and informational texts.

The type of organizational structure and the role structure plays in the text can vary greatly between literary and informational texts. For literary texts, students begin by learning how to examine the text for plot structure, identify the various parts of a literary text, and explain how different types of literature utilize different organizational structures. In older grades, students compare and contrast the structures of various texts and analyze how an author's choice of text structure affects the overall nature of the text.

The structure of informational texts is often more formal and explicit than literary texts. Students begin to learn about structure in informational texts by examining the presence and purpose of text features such as glossaries, headings, and table of contents. Later, they investigate the use of text structures such as compare/contrast, chronology, cause and effect, and problem/solution. They also analyze individual sections of writing (sentences, stanzas, paragraphs, etc.) in order to see how they contribute to the overall development of the text. By high school, students analyze the development of the author's claims or ideas in a text and evaluate the effectiveness of the text structure in achieving the author's goals.

Given the wide variety of text structures and features, it is especially important that students receive the necessary guidance and instruction in order to comprehend the complexities of structure. Text-dependent questions allow teachers to illustrate the numerous organizational structures and features used in text while simultaneously challenging their students to deepen their thinking and analysis skills regarding reading comprehension.

Text-Dependent Questions/Prompts

General Questions

- Does this text tell a story or give information? How do you know from the details in the text?

- How does this book/text differ from a book/text that gives information? Give specific examples from the text.

- How does this text differ from one that tells a story? Refer back to specific aspects of the text in your answer.

- What do you notice about the structure of this story? Use specific examples from the text to support your answer.

- How did the author choose to use dialogue in the story? What effect does the dialogue have? Include textual evidence in your answer.

Story Structure

- How does the author begin the story/act/passage/etc.? How does this beginning affect what happens in the middle of the story/act/passage/etc.? Be sure to cite the text to support your answer.

- What is the sequence of events in the story? Why is this important to the overall effect of the story?

- What event comes before/after _____ in the story? Why is this significant/important to the structure of the story?

- How and when does the author introduce the reader to the setting and characters in the story? Why do you think the author chose to structure the text this way?

- When does the author introduce the problem or conflict in the story? How does this timing affect the structure of the story?

- How does the author use text structure to introduce the story? Refer back to the text for evidence to support your answer.

- Does the story proceed chronologically/go in order? How do you know?

- How does the _____ sentence on page _____ contribute to the development of plot in the story?

- How does the author manipulate time in the story? What effect does this have for the reader? Support your answer with evidence from the text.

- Reread the first _____ sentences of the story. What is the purpose of these sentences? Why did the author choose to begin this way? Support your answer with specific examples from the text.

Text-Dependent Questions/Prompts (cont.)

Units of Text

- What structure does the author use to divide the text? Provide examples from the text. How does this structure affect the reader?

- How does each chapter/scene/stanza/etc. build on the one before it? Provide examples from the text in your answer.

- How does the dividing of the text into parts help the reader comprehend/ understand the story? Use specific examples to support your answer.

- Reread pages _____. How does this chapter/scene/stanza/etc. relate to the one that came before/after it?

- How do all of the text's individual parts (chapters, stanzas, scenes, etc.) come together to create a cohesive text? Refer back to the text in your answer.

- Reread the _____ sentence in the _____ paragraph. How does this sentence fit into the overall structure of the paragraph?

- What is the purpose of this scene in the structure of the play? Justify your answer with specific details from the text.

Types of Literature

- What type of literature is this text? How does the structure relate to the type of literature? Provide examples from the text to support your answer.

- Identify some of the structural elements in the poem using specific examples from the text.

- What form of poetry is this poem? How does its structure affect its meaning? Refer to specific words and phrases from the text in your answer.

- How does the structure of a drama differ from other types of literature? Give examples from the text to illustrate some of the structural elements present in drama.

Comparison and Evaluation

- Compare the structure of _____ to _____. How are the structures the same or different?

- What similarities do you see between the structure of _____ and _____? How do these similarities affect the style of the two texts? Include examples from the text in your answer.

- What differences do you see between the structure in _____ and _____? How do these differences play a role in the meanings of the two texts? Support your answer with specific details from the texts.

- Evaluate the effectiveness of the text structure using specific examples from the text.

Text-Dependent Questions/Prompts (cont.)

Text Features

- Reread the title of the story. How does the title connect to the rest of the story? Include specific words and phrases from the text in your answer.

- Reread the information in the text boxes. What purpose do these text boxes serve in the overall structure of the text? Use examples from the text to justify your answer.

- Review the headings used in the passage/chapter. How do these headings relate to the structure of the text? Refer to specific examples in the text to support your answer.

- What specific information does the heading on page _____ convey to the reader?

- Review the table of contents on page _____. Provide a specific example of how a reader would use this table of contents to gather information.

- Why did the author choose to include/use _____ (text feature) in the text? Explain your answer with examples from the text.

- What is the relationship between the heading on page _____ and the subheading on page _____?

- What is the purpose of the subtitle/heading _____? How does this text feature help the reader?

- Examine the words printed in *italics* or **bold** type. Why did the author choose to use this text feature for these words? Include specific words from the text as examples to support your answer.

- How does the heading _____ relate to the title _____?

- How could you use the index in this book to support your research on _____?

- What information is presented on the front and back cover of the book? Why was this information chosen to be on the cover?

- What new information did you learn from the _____ (text feature) in the _____ paragraph?

- What specific features of this text help the reader search for specific information?

- How do the text features used on page _____ relate to the topic of the text? Remember to use specific examples from the text to support your answer.

Text-Dependent Questions/Prompts *(cont.)*

Structure Type

- What type of structure does the author use in the text? How do you know? Include examples from the text to support your answer.

- Does this text tell a story or give information? How do you know from the structure of the text?

- What is being compared in the text? How is this reflected in the structure of the text? Use specific examples from the text to support your answer.

- What is the role of chronology in the text? Why do you think the author chose to use this type of structure to present information? Use specific examples from the text in your answer.

- How does _____ relate to _____ in the text? How does the text structure reflect this relationship?

- What is the problem presented in the text? What is the solution? Cite the text in your answer.

- What is the cause of _____ in the text? What are the effects of _____? Why did the author choose to use this type of structure in the text? Justify your answer with textual evidence.

- Does the text structure chosen by the author effectively communicate the information? Support your opinion with evidence from the text.

- Compare and contrast the structure used in _____ with the structure in _____. Which is more effective? Defend your answer with specific examples from the texts.

- How does the text structure help the reader gather information from the text? Include specific examples from the text in your answer.

Text Units

- Reread the _____ sentence/paragraph on page _____. How does this sentence/paragraph fit into the overall structure of the text?

- What is the role of chapter _____ in the development of the central concept of the text?

- How many major sections are there in the text? How are they related? Support your answer with textual evidence.

- What is the structure of the _____ paragraph on page _____? Analyze the role of each sentence in the paragraph.

- Reread the _____ paragraph on page _____. How does the first sentence relate to the last sentence?

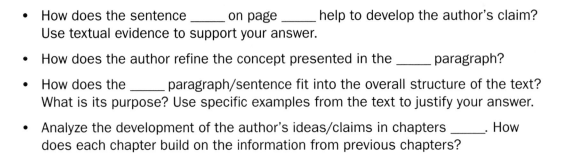

Text-Dependent Questions/Prompts *(cont.)*

- How does the sentence _____ on page _____ help to develop the author's claim? Use textual evidence to support your answer.

- How does the author refine the concept presented in the _____ paragraph?

- How does the _____ paragraph/sentence fit into the overall structure of the text? What is its purpose? Use specific examples from the text to justify your answer.

- Analyze the development of the author's ideas/claims in chapters _____. How does each chapter build on the information from previous chapters?

My Pets

I have a cat.

His name is Matt.

He likes to sit.

He likes to hide.

I have a dog.

His name is Tog.

He likes to play.

He likes to ride.

Tog and Matt

Have lots of fun,

When they play

In the hot, hot sun.

Matt will sit,

And Tog will ride,

As they romp around

With me outside.

Name: _____ Date: _____

My Pets (cont.)

Directions: Use the text to answer the questions below.

1 Does this text tell a story or give information? How do you know from the details in the text?

_____

- - - - - - - - - - - - - - -

_____

- - - - - - - - - - - - - - -

_____

- - - - - - - - - - - - - - -

_____

- - - - - - - - - - - - - - -

2 What type of text is this? Provide examples from the text to support your answer.

_____

- - - - - - - - - - - - - - -

_____

- - - - - - - - - - - - - - -

_____

- - - - - - - - - - - - - - -

Whales

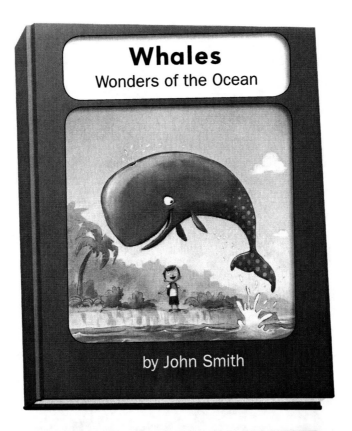

Whales
Wonders of the Ocean

by John Smith

Did you know that whales are the biggest animals on Earth? Whales live in the ocean. But they are not a fish. Whales are mammals. There are many different kinds of whales. Each type is different. Whales can hold their breath for a long time. They can also talk to each other. Whales are amazing!

Name: _____ Date: _____

Whales (cont.)

Directions: Use the text to answer the questions below.

1 What information is shown on the front and back cover of the book? Why was this information chosen to be on the covers?

_____

- -

_____

_____

- -

_____

_____

- -

_____

2 What is the purpose of the subtitle "Wonders of the Ocean"? How does this text feature help the reader?

_____

- -

_____

_____

- -

_____

_____

- -

_____

Excerpt from
Peter Rabbit
by Beatrix Potter

Once upon a time there were four little Rabbits. Their names were Flopsy, Mopsy, Cotton-tail, and Peter. They lived with their mother underneath a very big tree. "Now run and play," said Mrs. Rabbit one morning. "But remember, don't go into Mr. McGregor's garden."

Flopsy, Mopsy, and Cotton-tail were good little bunnies. They went down the path to gather blackberries. But Peter was very naughty. He ran straight away to Mr. McGregor's garden and squeezed under the gate! First he ate some lettuce and some beans. And then he went to look for some parsley. But at the end of the garden he ran into Mr. McGregor! Mr. McGregor was on his hands and knees planting cabbages. He jumped up and ran after Peter calling out, "Stop thief!" Peter was very scared. He rushed all over the garden looking for the gate.

Then Peter ran right into a net. The buttons on his jacket got caught in the net. Peter began to cry. Mr. McGregor came up with a bucket to trap Peter. But Peter wriggled out of the net just in time, leaving his jacket behind him. He rushed into the toolshed and jumped into a watering can. It would have been the perfect hiding place, except that it was filled with water. Mr. McGregor began to search through the toolshed. Then Peter sneezed—"Achoo!" Mr. McGregor was after him in no time.

Peter escaped by jumping through a window. The window was too small for Mr. McGregor. He was tired

Excerpt from
Peter Rabbit
by **Beatrix Potter** *(cont.)*

of running after Peter so he went back to his work. Peter sat down to rest. He was scared and wet.

Finally, Peter began to look around. He found a door in a wall, but it was locked. Peter began to cry again. Then he tried to find his way across the garden, but he became more and more lost. He went back towards the toolshed, but suddenly, he heard a noise. Peter hid underneath the bushes. After nothing happened, he came out, and climbed up on a wheelbarrow. He saw Mr. McGregor with his back towards Peter. Beyond Mr. McGregor was the gate! Peter got down very quietly and started running as fast as he could go. Mr. McGregor caught sight of him at the corner, but Peter did not care. He slipped under the gate, and was safe at last.

Peter ran all the way home to the big tree. He was so tired that he flopped down on the floor of the rabbit hole and shut his eyes. His mother was busy cooking. She wondered what he had done with his clothes. It was the second little jacket that Peter had lost!

I am sorry to say that Peter was not very well during that night. His mother put him to bed, but Flopsy, Mopsy, and Cotton-tail had bread and milk and blackberries for supper.

Name: _____ Date: _____

Excerpt from
Peter Rabbit
by Beatrix Potter *(cont.)*

Directions: Use the text to answer the questions below.

1 How does the author use text structure to introduce the story? Refer back to the text for evidence to support your answer.

_____

_____

_____

_____

2 How and when does the author introduce the reader to the setting and characters in the story? Why do you think the author chose to structure the text this way?

_____

_____

_____

_____

3 Reread the paragraph that starts with, "Then Peter ran right into a net." How does this paragraph fit into the overall structure of the text? Include examples from the text to support your answer.

_____

_____

_____

_____

Understanding Place Value

Some numbers have many digits. **Place value** shows the value of each digit. The place of the digit tells its value. Our number system is based on groups. We group by **tens**!

Fingers are called *digits*. We use fingers to count. Numbers are called *digits*, too. To find place value, look at each digit. Each place shows 10 times the place before it. See the chart. It shows how this works.

thousands	,	hundreds	tens	ones
10 x 100		10 x 10	10 x 1	
3	,	2	5	9

Different Ways to Write Numbers

See the number in the chart. We can write it as words. It is three thousand, two hundred fifty-nine. We can write it as digits. It is 3,259. The comma splits the number. It groups the digits by three. This makes it easy to read.

A zero holds a place. We use zero when there is no digit for that place. Think of 705. There are 7 groups of hundreds and there are 5 groups of ones. There are no groups of tens, so zero holds the tens place.

Place Value in Our Daily Lives

Place value helps us add, and it also helps us subtract. We have to line up the numbers by place value to make sure that we get the right answer. People who order supplies need to know about place value. They do not want to order too much or too little. A mistake could cost a lot of money! It is important to pay attention to place value.

Name: _____ Date: _____

Understanding Place Value (cont.)

Directions: Use the text to answer the questions below.

1 Why did the author choose to include words in *italics* in the text? Support your answer with examples from the text.

_____

_____

_____

_____

2 What new information did you learn from the **bold** words in the first paragraph?

_____

_____

_____

_____

3 How does the last paragraph fit into the overall structure of the text? What is its purpose? Use specific examples from the text to justify your answer.

_____

_____

_____

_____

Excerpt from

The Celebrated Jumping Frog of Calaveras County
by Mark Twain

You never see a frog so modest and straightfor'ard as he was. Though he was so gifted. And when it come to fair and square jumping on a dead level, he could get over more ground at one straddle than any animal of his breed you ever see. And when it come to that, Smiley would ante up money on him as long as he had a red. Smiley was monstrous proud of his frog.

One day a feller—a stranger in the camp, he was—come across Smiley with his frog. He says:

"What might be that you've got in the box?"

And Smiley says, sorter indifferent-like, "It might be a parrot, or it might be a canary, maybe. But it ain't—it's only just a frog."

And the feller took it. And he looked at it careful. And he turned it round this way and that. And he says, "H'm—so 'tis. Well, what's *he* good for?"

"Well," Smiley says, easy and careless, "he's good enough for *one* thing, I should judge. He can outjump any frog in Calaveras County."

"Well," he says the feller, "I don't see no p'ints about that frog that's any better'n any other frog."

"Maybe you don't," Smiley says, "but I've got *my* opinion. And I'll risk forty dollars that he can outjump any frog in Calaveras County."

And the feller studied a minute. Then he says, kinder sad like, "Well, I'm only a stranger here, and I ain't got no frog. But if I had a frog, I'd bet you."

And then Smiley says, "That's all right—if you'll hold my box a minute, I'll go and get you a frog." And so the feller took the box, put up his forty dollars along with Smiley's, and waited.

Eventually the feller got the frog out and prized his mouth open and took a teaspoon and filled him full of quail shot—filled him pretty near up to

Excerpt from
The Celebrated Jumping Frog of Calaveras County
by Mark Twain *(cont.)*

his chin—and set him on the floor. Smiley, he went to the swamp and ketched a frog and give him to this feller, and says:

"Now, if you're ready, set him alongside of Dan'l and I'll give the word." Then he says, "One-two-three-*git*!" and him and the feller touched up the frogs from behind, and the new frog hopped off lively, but Dan'l give a heave, and hysted up his shoulders, but he couldn't budge. Smiley was a surprised of course; he didn't have no idea what the matter was.

The feller took the money and when he was going out at the door, he says again, very deliberate, "Well," he says, "*I* don't see no p'ints about that frog that's any better'n any other frog."

Smiley, he stood scratching his head and looking down at Dan'l a long time. And at last he says, "I do wonder what in the nation that frog throwed off for. I wonder if there ain't something the matter with him. He 'pears to look mighty baggy, somehow." And he hefted Dan'l up by the nape of the neck and he turned him upside down and Dan'l belched out a double handful of shot. And then he was the maddest man—he set the frog down and took out after that feller, but he never ketched him.

Name: _____ Date: _____

Excerpt from
The Celebrated Jumping Frog of Calaveras County
by Mark Twain *(cont.)*

Directions: Use the text to answer the questions below.

1 How does this text differ from a text that gives information? Give specific examples from the text.

_____

_____

_____

2 How did the author choose to use dialogue in the story? What effect does the dialogue have on the overall text? Include textual evidence in your answer.

_____

_____

_____

3 What is the sequence of events in the story? Why is this important to the plot?

_____

_____

_____

4 Reread the first three sentences of the story. What is the purpose of these sentences? Why did the author choose to begin this way? Support your answer with specific examples from the text.

_____

_____

_____

#51449—TDQs: Strategies for Building Text-Dependent Questions   © Shell Education

Early American Indians in the Southwestern United States

There were many different early American Indian tribes. The Navajo, Apache, and Hopi tribes lived in the southwestern part of the United States. Each tribe had its own traditions and practices. Even though these tribes occupied the same general geographic regions, they were very different.

Navajo

The Navajo did not always live in the Southwest. They initially lived in Canada and Alaska. Over time, they traveled south and settled in the southwestern United States by the Pueblo Indians. They were known as nomadic people that moved frequently.

The Navajo built homes called **hogans**. These homes have wooden structures covered by tree bark and mud. They always faced east to welcome the morning sun. Hogans can have four sides or have a round shape like a cone. Many Navajo still live in hogans today.

The Navajo hunted deer and elk. They also farmed and gathered food. When the Spanish came to the Southwest, they brought sheep and horses. The Navajo learned how to use sheep wool to weave rugs and clothing. They also ate sheep for food. The Navajo used horses for transportation. They were able to travel farther to trade on horseback.

Apache

The Apache Indians were known for being hunters and warriors. These Indians were thought to be the fiercest fighters of all American Indians. Apache Indians were very skilled at riding horses. Horses were an important part of their culture.

The Apache lived in small groups of five to ten families called **bands**. These bands moved together several times a year. They moved between various campgrounds as necessary. The family huts were called **wickiups**. These structures were made from wooden sticks and grass. Wickiups were short, squat structures.

Early American Indians in the Southwestern United States (cont.)

The Apaches were not farmers. The men hunted food with bows and arrows. Raiding was also part of Apache life. Apache braves often raided ranches and wagon trains for supplies they could use. The women gathered fruit, nuts, and berries to eat. Food was shared with the whole camp.

Hopi

The Hopi Indians were a very peaceful tribe. They were not warriors and did not like to fight. The Hopi were excellent farmers. They grew beans, pumpkins, melon, and much more. Corn was their most important crop. The Hopi have many religious ceremonies that center around corn because it is so important to them.

The Hopi built their homes out of **adobe**. The homes were stacked and the Hopi used ladders to reach the different levels. The Hopi made beautiful woven baskets and clay pottery. They also wove fabric and made silver jewelry. Many Hopi continue these artistic traditions today.

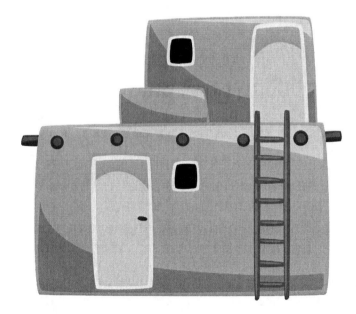

Name: _____   Date: _____

Early American Indians in the Southwestern United States *(cont.)*

Directions: Use the text to answer the questions below.

1 How does the text structure help the reader gather information from the text? Include specific examples from the text in your answer.

_____

_____

_____

2 How does the heading *Navajo* relate to the title "Early American Indians in the Southwestern United States"?

_____

_____

_____

3 Reread the last sentence in the first paragraph. How does this sentence support the overall structure of the text?

_____

_____

_____

4 What is being compared in the text? How is this reflected in the structure of the text? Use specific examples from the text to support your answer.

_____

_____

_____

Excerpt from
Macbeth
by William Shakespeare, Act I, Scene VII

Macbeth: If I am going to murder the king, I resolve to act quickly. I cannot allow myself to pause or to think about what I am doing, because then I will only feel guilt about my actions. If I kill him, I will become king, and being king is what I want. Instead of considering the horrific acts I must commit to become king, I must focus on how great I will feel when I am finally am king. King Duncan is here as a guest in my house, and as a guest, he should be treated with honor and generosity. He is a loyal friend, a wise and just king, a strong and responsible commander, and he has always treated me with respect. Even this week, he has bestowed a great honor on me, and I would repay his trust in me by taking his life for no other reason than to steal his power. Part of me feels such extreme guilt for contemplating the murder of any kind. But another part of me craves the power he has and will do whatever is necessary to have it. Which part of me will win this battle?

Enter Lady Macbeth

My wife, what is the news of King Duncan?

Lady Macbeth: He is almost done eating his dinner, but why are you here when we agreed that you would hide in his room?

Macbeth: Has King Duncan asked where I am?

Lady Macbeth: Why would he do that?

Macbeth: I do not want to do this anymore. Duncan is a noble and worthy king, he does not deserve this cruelty we are planning. If I am meant to be king, I should simply wait for the title to come to me in its own time.

Lady Macbeth: How can you say that, my husband, when we both decided last night that you would take Duncan's life? You had such unshakable hope in yourself when we devised our plan and believed in the signs that indicated that now, this moment, is the time to act. Have you become afraid and fearful of your desire to be king? Are you willing to live your entire life never having the courage to take what you want?

Macbeth: Stop this mean-spirited speech. I have acted always with bravery and integrity in every battle I have fought, for any man who takes a wicked and selfish action for himself and not for what is right is not a real man.

Lady Macbeth: So last night when we planned this, you were not a man? We spoke to each other of our dreams for the future, and you told me you knew it was your destiny to be king. So together, we created a plan to make that dream come true. Last night, you did not seem to mind what that meant for King Duncan, and how can he matter now when we are so close to getting what we want? If I were you, I would be able to do what we planned, and I would be willing to sacrifice anything to get you what you wanted, even if that meant throwing my own child away.

Name: _____ Date: _____

Excerpt from
Macbeth
by William Shakespeare, Act I, Scene VII *(cont.)*

Directions: Use the text to answer the questions below.

1 What type of literature is this text? How does the structure relate to the type of literature? Provide examples from the text to support your answer.

_____

_____

_____

_____

2 How does the author begin the Act? How does this beginning relate to what happens in the middle of the Act? Cite the text to support your answer.

_____

_____

_____

_____

3 When does the author introduce the problem or conflict in the passage? How does this timing affect the structure of the text?

_____

_____

_____

_____

4 What do you think is the purpose of this scene in the structure of the play? Justify your answer with specific details from the text.

_____

_____

_____

_____

Our Wondrous Solar System

The solar system is a huge area in space. It is the home of eight planets and more than 160 moons. You can also find dwarf planets and tons of asteroids in the solar system. The night sky has been an object of curiosity and fascination throughout history. The ancient Greeks looked into the night sky just as you do and they saw objects that seemed to wander around the sky over the course of a year. They used the Greek word *planetes*, which means "wanderer." Today, we know that these wandering objects are planets.

Ancient astronomers once thought Earth was the center of the solar system. They said that everything else in the sky, including the sun, orbited around Earth. This view is known as *geocentrism* and people believed it until four hundred years ago. Galileo Galilei was the first astronomer to claim that Earth was not the center. He proved the sun is the center of the solar system, a view known as *heliocentrism*. Today, we know the planets revolve around the sun in elliptical orbits.

Scientists divide planets into three main groups. The first group is called the *terrestrial planets* and is consists of Mercury, Venus, Earth, and Mars. These planets are also known as the *inner planets* because they are closest to the sun. They are also distinguishable by their solid rocky surfaces.

The second group of planets, the outer planets, consists of Jupiter, Saturn, Uranus, and Neptune. This group is also called the *Jovian planets* or *gas giants*. These planets are much bigger than Earth; you could fit 1,321 Earths inside Jupiter! Gas giants do not have a solid surface because they are made primarily of gas. Some of these planets, such as Neptune and Uranus, are made of ice and gas. They are sometimes called *ice giants*.

The third group of planets is called the *dwarf planets*. These are bodies in space that are similar to planets, but they do not meet all of the criteria to be a planet. For more than 70 years, Pluto was listed as the ninth planet of the solar system. Then in 2006, scientists came up with a new definition for a planet. Suddenly, Pluto did not fit that definition so it was demoted and is now considered a dwarf planet.

Besides the planets, there are many other bodies in the solar system. First, there are the moons orbiting the planets. Earth has just one moon, but other planets have dozens of them. Mercury and Venus do not have any moons at all. There is also a part of the solar system known as the Asteroid Belt. It is between Mars and Jupiter and it made up of many oddly shaped rocks.

What is beyond our wondrous solar system? Are there other planets in space where life exists? Those are questions that astronomers are exploring today.

Name: _____   Date: _____

Our Wondrous Solar System *(cont.)*

Directions: Use the text to answer the questions below.

1 Why did the author choose to include *italics* in the text? Explain your answer using examples from the text.

_____

_____

_____

_____

2 What is the structure of the second paragraph in the text? Analyze the role of each sentence in the paragraph.

_____

_____

_____

_____

3 How does the author refine the concept presented in the fifth paragraph?

_____

_____

_____

_____

4 How do moons relate to the solar system in the text? How does the text structure reflect this relationship?

_____

_____

_____

_____

Excerpt from
Crime and Punishment, Part I, Chapter I
by Fyodor Dostoevsky

On an exceptionally hot and humid evening early in July a young man came out of the garret in which he lodged in S. Place and walked slowly, as though in hesitation, towards K. bridge.

He had successfully avoided meeting his landlady on the staircase. His garret under the roof of the high, five-storied house was more like a cupboard than a room and the landlady, who provided him with garret, dinners, and attendance, lived on the floor below, and every time he went out he was obliged to pass her kitchen, the door of which invariably stood open. And each time he passed, the young man had a sick, frightened feeling, which made him scowl and feel ashamed. He was hopelessly in debt to his landlady, and was afraid of meeting her.

This was not because he was cowardly and abject, quite the contrary; but for some time past he had been in an overstrained irritable condition, verging on hypochondria. He had become so completely absorbed in himself, and isolated from his fellows that he dreaded meeting, not only his landlady, but anyone at all. He was crushed by poverty, but the anxieties of his position had of late ceased to weigh upon him. He had given up attending to matters of practical importance; he had lost all desire to do so. Nothing that any landlady could do had a real terror for him. But to be stopped on the stairs, to be forced to listen to her trivial, irrelevant gossip, to pestering demands for payment, threats and complaints, and to rack his brains for excuses, to prevaricate, to lie—no, rather than that, he would creep down the stairs like a cat and slip out unseen.

This evening, however, on coming out into the street, he became acutely aware of his fears.

"I want to attempt a thing *like that* and am frightened by these trifles," he thought, with an odd smile. "Hm... yes, all is in a man's hands and he lets it all slip from cowardice, that's an axiom; it would be interesting to know what it is men are most afraid of.... But I am talking too much. It's because I chatter that I do nothing, or perhaps it is that I chatter because I do nothing. I've learned to chatter this last month, lying for days together in my den thinking... of Jack the Giant-killer. Why am I going there now and am I capable of *that*? It's simply a fantasy to amuse myself; a plaything!"

The heat in the street was terrible: and the airlessness, the bustle and the plaster, scaffolding, bricks, and dust all about him, and that special Petersburg stench, so familiar to all who are unable to get out of town in summer—all worked painfully upon the young man's already overwrought nerves. The insufferable stench from the pot-houses, which are particularly numerous in that part of the town, and the drunken men whom he met continually, although it was a working day, completed the revolting misery of the picture. An expression of the profoundest disgust gleamed for a moment in the young man's refined face. He was, by the way, exceptionally handsome, above the average in height, slim, well-built, with beautiful dark eyes and dark brown hair. Soon he sank into deep thought, or more accurately speaking into a complete blankness of mind;

Excerpt from
Crime and Punishment, Part I, Chapter I
by Fyodor Dostoevsky *(cont.)*

he walked along not observing what was about him and not caring to observe it. From time to time, he would mutter something, from the habit of talking to himself, to which he had just confessed. At these moments he would become conscious that his ideas were sometimes in a tangle and that he was very weak for he had scarcely tasted food for two days.

He was so badly dressed that even a man accustomed to shabbiness would have been ashamed to be seen in the street in such rags. In that quarter of the town, however, scarcely any shortcoming in dress would have created surprise. Owing to the proximity of the Hay Market, the number of establishments of bad character, the preponderance of the trading and working class population crowded in these streets and alleys in the heart of Petersburg, types so various were to be seen in the streets that no figure, however odd, would have caused surprise. But there was such accumulated bitterness and contempt in the young man's heart, that, in spite of all the fastidiousness of youth, he minded his rags least of all in the street. It was a different matter when he met with acquaintances or with former fellow students, whom, indeed, he disliked meeting at any time. And yet when a drunken man who, for some unknown reason, was being taken somewhere in a huge wagon dragged by a heavy dray horse, suddenly shouted at him as he drove past: "Hey there, German hatter" bawling at the top of his voice and pointing at him—the young man stopped suddenly and clutched tremulously at his hat. It was a tall round hat from Zimmerman's, but completely worn out, rusty with age, all torn and bespattered, brimless and bent on one side in a most unseemly fashion. Not shame, however, but quite another feeling akin to terror had overtaken him.

"I knew it," he muttered in confusion, "I thought so! That's the worst of all! Why, a stupid thing like this, the most trivial detail might spoil the whole plan. Yes, my hat is too noticeable.... It looks absurd and that makes it noticeable.... With my rags I ought to wear a cap, any sort of old pancake, but not this grotesque thing. Nobody wears such a hat, it would be noticed a mile off, it would be remembered.... What matters is that people would remember it, and that would give them a clue. For this business one should be as little conspicuous as possible.... Trifles, trifles are what matter! Why, it's just such trifles that always ruin everything...."

He had not far to go; he knew indeed how many steps it was from the gate of his lodging house: exactly seven hundred and thirty. He had counted them once when he had been lost in dreams. At the time he had put no faith in those dreams and was only tantalising himself by their hideous but daring recklessness. Now, a month later, he had begun to look upon them differently, and, in spite of the monologues in which he jeered at his own impotence and indecision, he had involuntarily come to regard this "hideous" dream as an exploit to be attempted, although he still did not realise this himself. He was positively going now for a "rehearsal" of his project, and at every step his excitement grew more and more violent.

Name: _____ Date: _____

Excerpt from
Crime and Punishment, Part I, Chapter I
by Fyodor Dostoevsky *(cont.)*

Directions: Use the text to answer the questions below.

1 How does the author begin the passage? How does this beginning affect what happens in the middle of the passage? Cite the text to support your answer.

_____

_____

_____

_____

2 How did the author choose to use dialogue in the passage? What effect does the dialogue have? Include textual evidence in your answer.

_____

_____

_____

_____

3 Reread the paragraph that starts with, "The heat in the street was terrible." How does this paragraph fit into the overall structure of the text? What is its purpose? Include examples from the text to support your answer.

_____

_____

_____

_____

4 Evaluate the effectiveness of the text structure using specific examples from the text.

_____

_____

_____

_____

#51449—TDQs: Strategies for Building Text-Dependent Questions

Excerpt from
The Byzantine Empire: A Society that Shaped the World
by Kelly Rodgers

A Divided Empire

The Roman Empire was one of the world's first superpowers. During its peak, it controlled parts of Europe, Asia, and Africa. In the first century, nearly 54 million people lived in the Roman Empire. Rome, the capital, was one of the largest and grandest cities in the world.

By the end of the third century, the empire was in trouble because powerful invaders were threatening its borders. The economy was weak and many leaders were corrupt. As a result, this period became known as the Crisis of the Third Century.

Too Many Emperors

The Crisis of the Third Century lasted from AD 235 to 285. One of the problems during this time was leadership because there were more than 20 different emperors. Most of these emperors ruled for just a few months.

Emperor Diocletian made an important decision when he decided to divide the empire in two. He hoped this would make it easier to rule. Diocletian ruled the Eastern Roman Empire and a different emperor ruled the Western Roman Empire. The Western Roman Empire survived, but not well, while the Eastern Roman Empire became strong and powerful. Diocletian had laid the foundation for the future.

The Eastern Roman Empire is known today as the Byzantine Empire and, under leaders such as Constantine and Justinian I, the empire flourished. The Byzantine preserved the treasures of the ancient world and they created a unique culture. Lasting for over a thousand years, the Byzantine Empire shaped the world.

Roman or Byzantine?

People who lived in the Byzantine Empire did not call their empire by that name. They thought of themselves as Romans and it was not until the 18th century that the term *Byzantine* was used to describe the empire.

Emperor Constantine

Attacking the West

Diocletian was worried about choosing a successor to take over as the new emperor. He did not think that sons should take over leadership from their fathers and at the time, no one considered women to be fit leaders. Diocletian thought emperors should be chosen based on their ability to lead. He created a **tetrarchy**, or a system with four rulers where each of the two Roman Empires

Excerpt from
The Byzantine Empire: A Society that Shaped the World
by Kelly Rodgers *(cont.)*

had an Augustus, or senior emperor, and a Caesar, or junior emperor. He decided that when an emperor stepped down, the Caesar would become the new Augustus and then a new Caesar would be chosen, but his plan did not work.

Diocletian's successor died in 306 and then the successor's son, Constantine, took over as emperor instead of the Augustus. That same year, Maxentius, the son of a former emperor, wanted the power that Constantine claimed. When Maxentius's father died, Maxentius took the role of the emperor even though he was not the Caesar. In 312, Constantine decided to attack Maxentius because he wanted to control the Western Empire. The two armies met in Rome at the Tiber River by the Milvian Bridge. Even though he was not a Christian, Constantine prayed to the Christian God for victory and he had his men make banners bearing the Christian cross. Constantine's men carried the banners into battle and won. His decision to fight under the banner of Christianity would change the course of world history.

Attacking the East

The tetrarchy had failed. A system that was designed to reward merit was being changed to promote the son of a former Augustus. After several battles and deaths, it came down to Constantine and Emperor Licinius. Emperor Licinius had taken over much of the eastern territories and had become sole emperor. Constantine wanted to defeat Licius, regain the East, and control the Roman Empire.

In 324, the armies of Licinius and Constantine fought near the ancient Greek city of Byzantium and Constantine's men won the battle. Once again, the Roman Empire was united under one emperor, Constantine the Great.

Feudalism

Due to all the fighting, the Roman Empire's economy grew weak and it became hard for people to make enough money to live. Constantine made several changes to get people back to work and help improve the economy. He forced peasants to stay on their land and farm and he made sons do the same works as their fathers. These changes led to a new social and economic system called **feudalism**.

Since Rome was far away from the main population centers of the East, Constantine wanted to build a new capital closer to the middle of the empire. He thought the old Greek city of Byzantium was the perfect place because the site overlooked the battleground where he had reunited the empire. More importantly, it was situated on the main trade route between the Black Sea and the Mediterranean Sea and, since it was surrounded on three sides by water, it would be easy to defend. He called the new city Constantinople. For many years, Constantinople went on to be one of the most successful and beautiful cities in the entire world.

Name: _____ Date: _____

Excerpt from
The Byzantine Empire: A Society that Shaped the World
by Kelly Rodgers *(cont.)*

Directions: Use the text to answer the questions below.

1 What is the role of chronology in the text? Why do you think the author chose to use this type of structure to present information? Refer back to specific examples from the text.

_____

_____

_____

_____

2 Review the headings used in the passage. How do these headings relate to the structure of the text? Refer to specific examples in the text to support your answer.

_____

_____

_____

_____

3 Examine the words printed in **bold** type. Why did the author choose to use this text feature for these words? Include examples from the text to support your answer.

_____

_____

_____

_____

4 How does dividing the text into parts help the reader understand the information? Use specific examples to support your answer.

_____

_____

_____

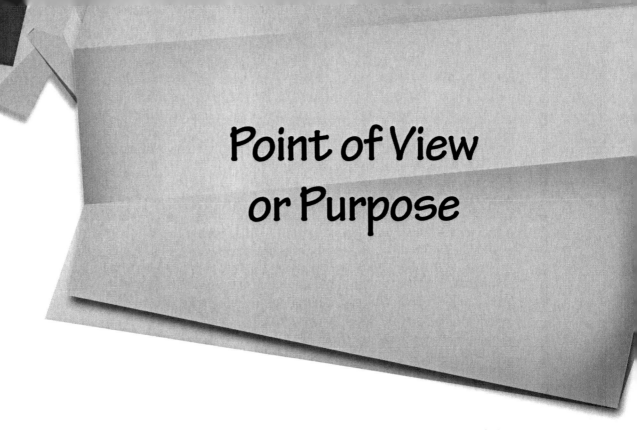

Point of View or Purpose

Text-dependent questions (TDQs) are important to the understanding of point of view or purpose. In this section, you will find an overview, sample text-dependent questions/prompts, literary and informational passages, as well as supporting questions/prompts to use with your students. Below is a chart that provides the titles and the recommended grade ranges for the texts in this section.

Grade Range	Literary Text	Page #	Informational Text	Page #
K–1	*I Don't Want To...*	195	*Ice Cream Sundaes*	197
2–3	Excerpt from *My Father's Dragon* by Ruth Stiles Gannett	199	*Inside Land Biomes*	202
4–5	Excerpt from *King Lear, Act I Scene I,* by William Shakespeare	205	*Corps of Discovery*	208
6–8	Excerpt from *The Heart of Darkness* by Joseph Conrad	210	*Rotations in Geometry*	212
9–12	Excerpt from *Frankenstein, or the Modern Prometheus* by Mary Wollstonecraft Shelley	214	Excerpt from *Women and War Work* by Helen Fraser	217

#51449—TDQs: Strategies for Building Text-Dependent Questions

Point of View or Purpose Overview

People read texts for a variety of reasons. Novels are often read for entertainment, pleasure, and relaxation. Instruction manuals and nonfiction books serve educational and practical purposes. Road signs and warning labels help keep people safe. Regardless of the type of writing, it is important that the reader be able to recognize the purpose of the text. By understanding the purpose of the text, the reader is better equipped to comprehend its message and absorb the pertinent information presented.

In addition, it is also important that readers be able to evaluate an author's point of view. According to Pasch and Norsworthy (2001), "the ability to identify and recognize the importance of point of view is one of the cornerstones of critical thinking" (20). Rather than simply accepting the information in a given text as fact, readers need to understand that every author presents his or her ideas from a particular point of view. An author's point of view affects the way in which a story is told, an event is related, or an idea is described. Text dependent questions help students identify the purpose and point of view of a text by highlighting important aspects of the text and illustrating the development of these important literary elements.

The Common Core State Standards (2010) address the relevance of purpose and point of view in the sixth reading standard. This standard states that students should be able to, "assess how point of view or purpose shapes the content and style of a text." With literature, students start by examining the role of the author and illustrator in the telling of the story. In later grades, students learn to identify the narrator and describe the viewpoints of the various characters in the text. They learn to differentiate between their personal point of view and that of the author, compare and contrast first- and third-person narrations, and analyze the development of point of view over the course of a text. Ultimately, high school students need to describe how the author uses point of view to develop literary effects, such as irony or satire, within the text.

With informational texts, students must be able to determine the purpose of the text "including what the author wants to answer, explain, or describe." They learn to distinguish the author's point of view from their own, as well as compare and contrast multiple accounts of the same event. In the upper grades, students build on this knowledge by examining how the author distinguishes his or her point of view from that of others and how he or she uses rhetoric and specific language to advance this point of view.

Determining the purpose of a text and identifying an author's point of view are complex skills that require study and practice to master. In most texts, neither the purpose of the text nor the point of view is explicitly stated, making it the student's responsibility to extract the necessary information to make this determination. Text-dependent questions serve as excellent guides to help students identify the appropriate information, determine the purpose, and analyze the role of the author's point of view in the text.

Text-Dependent Questions/Prompts

Point of View

- Who is the author of the book? Who is the illustrator? What are their roles in telling the story/presenting information?

- Describe one thing you learned from the picture that is not in the text.

- How does the information in the picture/illustration/map contribute to/support the information presented/shown in the text?

- Who is telling the story? How do you know? Use examples from the text to support your answer.

- Who narrates the story at the beginning? Middle? End? Use text examples to show how you know this information.

- How many different narrators are there in the text? Why do you think the author chose to use multiple narrators? Support your answer with evidence from the text.

- What effect does the use of multiple narrators have on the overall tone and message of the text? Provide examples from the text to support your answer.

- Describe the different points of view of each character in the story. Use specific words and phrases from the text to support your answer.

- What is _____'s point of view in the text? How do you know? Use examples from the text to support your answer.

- How does _____'s point of view differ from _____'s point of view? Support your answer with examples from the text.

- How does the author use different viewpoints to enhance the development of the characters in the story?

- What role does point of view play in the development of theme over the course of the story?

- How do the characters' points of view contribute to the conflict and resolution in the story? Justify your answer with examples from the text.

- How is _____'s viewpoint expressed through the dialogue in the text?

- What is the narrator's point of view in the poem? How do you know?

- What is the author's point of view on the topic of _____? Provide evidence from the text to support your answer.

- How does your point of view differ from that of the narrator/characters in the text? Give examples from the text to illustrate the differences.

- How is your point of view the same or different from the author's? Use evidence from the text to show these similarities and differences.

- Compare and contrast the differences in point of view between the story of _____ and _____. Include examples from the texts to support your answer.

Text-Dependent Questions/Prompts (cont.)

- Does this story use first- or third-person narration? How do you know? Use examples from the text to support your answer.

- Why did the author chose to use first-/third-person perspective in this story? Support your answer with specific details from the text.

- Is the narrator in this story omniscient? What language in the text tells you this information?

- How does the author use point of view to draw the reader into the story?

- How does the narrator's/speaker's point of view influence the description of the events that occur in the story?

- How does the author develop the narrator's/speaker's point of view over the course of the text?

- How do _____'s actions depict his/her viewpoint in the text?

- How does the author use _____'s dialogue to express his/her point of view?

- How does the author develop the point of view of ____ over the course of the text?

- What are the similarities between _____'s and _____'s points of view? What are the differences?

- How does the author establish separate points of view between the audience/reader and the narrator/speaker through the text? Include examples from the text to support your answer.

- How does the author use different points of view to create humor/suspense/tension/etc. in the text?

- How does the author use point of view to convey emotion to the audience/reader?

- How is the narrator's/author's cultural perspective highlighted in the point of view of the text?

- Analyze how _____'s point of view in the text reflects his/her culture.

- How does the author develop _____'s point of view without explicitly stating it in the text?

- What literary techniques does the author use to develop the point of view of _____ in the text? Support you answer with examples from the text.

- How does the author distinguish his/her point of view or purpose from that of others?

Text-Dependent Questions/Prompts (cont.)

- Does the author acknowledge others' points of view in the text? How so? Include examples from the text to support your answer.

- What are the conflicting viewpoints presented in the text?

- How does the author respond to evidence that conflicts with his/her viewpoint in the text?

- What language does the author use to advance his/her viewpoint? Is the use of this language effective? Use specific words and phrases from the text to justify your answer.

Purpose

- What is the main purpose of the text? Support your answer with evidence from the text.

- What is the question that the author is trying to answer in the text?

- What does the author want the reader to understand through the text? Provide examples from the text to support your answer.

- What are the similarities and differences between the firsthand account of _____ and the secondhand account?

- Does the author accomplish his/her purpose in the text? Provide examples and details from the text to support your opinion.

- Compare and contrast _____'s and _____'s account of _____. What are the similarities and/or differences in focus?

- Is the information provided in the two accounts of _____ the same or different? Use examples from the text to support your answer.

- How does the author convey his/her purpose in the text? Be sure to include specific words and phrases from the text in your answer.

- What is the author's purpose in the text? How does he/she use rhetoric to establish and advance his/her position?

- What specific language does the author use to persuade the reader?

- How do the style and content of the text contribute to the author's purpose?

I Don't Want To...

I don't want to get up today.

I want to stay in bed all day.

I hear my mom coming up the stairs.

I close my eyes and pretend that I am asleep.

Maybe she will think that I am sick.

Maybe she will say that I need to stay home today.

Name: _____   Date: _____

I Don't Want To... (cont.)

Directions: Use the text to answer the questions below.

1 What did you learn from the words in the story? What did you learn from the illustration?

_____

_____

_____

_____

_____

_____

_____

_____

2 Who is telling the story? How do you know?

_____

_____

_____

_____

_____

Ice Cream Sundaes

Ice cream sundaes are the best dessert.

First, you pick the flavor of ice cream. Sometimes you even get more than one flavor.

Then, you get to choose a sauce. My favorite is chocolate. Caramel is really good, too.

Next, you add the toppings. There are lots of toppings. Some people like fruit or nuts. Some like candy. I always choose sprinkles.

Then, you add whipped cream. Last is a cherry on the top.

Nothing can beat an ice cream sundae!

Name: _____ Date: _____

Ice Cream Sundaes (cont.)

Directions: Use the text to answer the questions below.

1 Write one thing you learned from the picture that is not in the text.

_____

- -
_____

- -
_____

- -
_____

2 What is the main purpose of the text? Support your answer with examples from the text.

_____

- -
_____

- -
_____

- -
_____

- -
_____

Excerpt from
My Father's Dragon
by Ruth Stiles Gannett

The tigers walked around him in a big circle. Every second they looked hungrier. And then they sat down and they began to talk. "I bet you thought we didn't know you were here! You are in our jungle without our say so! That is trespassing!"

Then the next tiger spoke. "I bet you will say you didn't know it was our jungle!"

"Not one explorer has ever left this island alive!" said the third tiger. My father thought of the old alley cat so he knew this wasn't true. But he had too much sense to say so. One doesn't argue with a hungry tiger.

The tigers went on talking. Each took a turn. "You're our first little boy. I'm curious. I wonder if you are extra tender."

"Maybe you think we have regular meal-times, but we do not. We eat whenever we feel hungry," said the fifth tiger.

"And we are very hungry right now. In fact, I can hardly wait," said the sixth.

"I can't wait!" said the seventh tiger.

Then all the tigers spoke together. They roared, "Let us start right now!" And they moved in closer.

Excerpt from
My Father's Dragon
by Ruth Stiles Gannett *(cont.)*

My father looked and he saw those seven hungry tigers. And he had an idea. He opened his knapsack and he took out the chewing gum. The alley cat had told him that tigers really like gum and it was very rare on the island. So he threw a piece to each one, but they only growled. "We do like gum, but we are sure we would like you even better!" They moved closer. They were so close that he could feel them breathing on his face.

"But this is very special gum," said my father. "Keep chewing it long enough and it will turn green and then you can plant it and it will grow more! The sooner you start the sooner you will have more."

The tigers said, "Why, you don't say! Isn't that fine!" Each one wanted to be the first to plant the gum so they all unwrapped their pieces and began chewing. They chewed as hard as they could. Every once in a while one tiger would look into another's mouth. He would say, "Nope, it's not done yet." Soon, they were all busy looking into each other's mouths. They wanted to make sure that no one was getting ahead. They forgot all about my father!

Name: _____ Date: _____

Excerpt from
My Father's Dragon
by Ruth Stiles Gannett *(cont.)*

Directions: Use the text to answer the questions below.

1 Who is telling the story? How do you know? Use examples from the text to support your answer.

_____

_____

_____

_____

2 How is the tigers' viewpoint expressed through the dialogue in the text?

_____

_____

_____

_____

3 Why did the author choose to use first-person perspective in the story? Support your answer with specific details from the text.

_____

_____

_____

_____

Inside Land Biomes

What Is a Biome?

Earth has different areas called **biomes**. Each biome has its own climate. This affects the kinds of plants and animals that can live there.

Altitude and **latitude** define where a biome is located. Altitude measures how high a place is. It measures the height above sea level. It affects what can grow. Latitude tells how hot a place is. It measures how far away a place is from the **equator**. The equator is an invisible line around the middle of Earth. The closer to the equator, the hotter the weather gets. The farther away from the equator, the cooler the weather gets.

Types of Biomes

At the top of the world, the weather is very cold. This biome is called **tundra**. Strong, cold winds sweep across the flat tundra. The top layer of soil freezes in winter. It thaws in the summer. Only grasses, lichens, and mosses can grow there. Some tundra animals are caribou, wolves, and snowy owls.

Just south of the tundra is the largest land biome. It is called **taiga**. Winters are long and cold. Summers are short and cool. Evergreen trees grow in the taiga. They do not lose their leaves in the winter. Grizzly bears, eagles, and deer live there. The taiga also has lakes, bogs, and rivers.

#51449—TDQs: Strategies for Building Text-Dependent Questions

Inside Land Biomes (cont.)

A little farther south, the weather warms up. There are four seasons. This is the **temperate forest**. Maple, beech, and oak trees are found there. Deer, raccoons, foxes, and squirrels also make their homes in these forests. Many people do, too.

Near the equator, it is near 77°F year-round. This is where you will find **tropical rainforests**. This biome has millions of different plants and animals. Tropical rainforests cover less than 7 percent of the land on Earth. Yet they support more than half Earth's plant and animal species!

The **grassland** has hot, dry summers. There are mild, wet winters, too. Grasslands cover one-fourth of Earth's land. There are evergreen bushes that never grow over 10 feet tall. It does not rain often in grasslands.

Some places on Earth hardly ever get rain. This biome is called **desert**. Most deserts are hot. During the day, it may reach 121°F in the shade! Then, at night, it can be close to freezing. Desert plants have adapted to these harsh conditions. To avoid the heat, most desert animals sleep during the day and come out at night.

Name: _____   Date: _____

Inside Land Biomes (cont.)

Directions: Use the text to answer the questions below.

1 What is the main purpose of the text? Support your answer with evidence from the text.

_____

_____

_____

_____

2 What does the author want the reader to understand through the text? Provide examples from the text to support your answer.

_____

_____

_____

_____

3 How do the style and content of the text contribute to the author's purpose?

_____

_____

_____

_____

Excerpt from
King Lear, Act I, Scene I,
by William Shakespeare

King Lear: And now we can speak about the reason we are all gathered together. Hand me that map of our kingdom. You can see here that I have drawn lines to divide the land into three parts. I am an old man and the time has come for me to stop working so hard. I want to pass onto my three lovely daughters the responsibilities of this kingdom. They are young, strong, and smart and will ensure that the kingdom lasts long into the future. I have great power to hand over today, and to ensure that the right daughter wins that power, I have a plan. The daughter who pleases me the most will earn the biggest reward. Each daughter will come and tell me how much she loves me, and the daughter who can convince me that her love is the greatest will get the largest piece of land. Now, Goneril, the oldest of my daughters, come forward and speak.

Goneril: Father, I love you more than I can tell you. There are no words powerful enough in the wide world to express how deep and rich my love is for you.

Cordelia: [Aside] What can I say when it is my turn? I love him with more honesty than my selfish sisters, but they will say anything to get the power he is handing out. I shall love him as I always have in my heart, but I will not play this game of lies.

King Lear: That is a wonderful answer, Goneril, and for it I will give you this rich piece of land. It has deep forests for hunting, vast meadows for planting, and rushing rivers of delicious water. Now, Regan, my second daughter, come forward and tell me how much you love me.

Excerpt from
King Lear, Act I, Scene I,
by William Shakespeare *(cont.)*

Regan: Father, I love you with just as much passion as Goneril. I want nothing but to make you happy. Your approval is all that I want in this world. I would turn away anyone who does not work for your pleasure.

Cordelia: [Aside] My sisters are cruel liars. They say this only to grab the land and money our father is foolishly giving away.

King Lear: And I will be your happy father knowing you love me this much. To you, I will give this other piece of land that has just as much richness and beauty as the piece I gave to Goneril. Now Cordelia, my third, my youngest, my most favorite daughter, come and tell me how much you love me.

Cordelia: I have nothing to say, Father.

King Lear: Nothing?

Cordelia: Nothing.

King Lear: If you say nothing, you will get nothing. Think carefully, and then speak of your love for me.

Cordelia: I wish that my heart could speak of all the love I have there for you, but it cannot, and I will not speak fake words of love to my own father. It would be disrespectful and unkind, and I will not do it.

Name: _____ Date: _____

Excerpt from
King Lear, Act I, Scene I,
by William Shakespeare *(cont.)*

Directions: Use the text to answer the questions below.

1 Who is telling the story? How do you know?

_____

_____

_____

_____

2 How does the author use different viewpoints to enhance the development of the characters in the story?

_____

_____

_____

3 How is Cordelia's viewpoint expressed through the dialogue in the text?

_____

_____

_____

4 How does the author use different points of view to create suspense in the text?

_____

_____

_____

Corps of Discovery

In 1803, President Thomas Jefferson made the best land deal ever! At the time, Napoleon Bonaparte was the leader of France. Napoleon experienced many problems after he took the French throne. There was a slave revolt in Haiti, which was controlled by France. Napoleon lost many soldiers in his effort to stop the revolt. It also cost France a lot of money. At this time, France controlled a piece of land west of the United States. This land was called Louisiana. It stretched north and west of the Mississippi River. Napoleon needed money to prepare for war with Europe. He agreed to sell the Louisiana Territory to the United States for 15 million dollars. That's three cents an acre! This was known as the Louisiana Purchase.

At this time, two out of three people lived near the Atlantic Ocean in the East. No one from the United States had explored the West. Jefferson wanted to control the whole continent. He wanted to find the Northwest Passage, which would connect the Atlantic and Pacific Oceans. He asked his secretary, Meriwether Lewis, to explore this new land that the United States had purchased.

Lewis grew up in Virginia. He had known Thomas Jefferson for his whole life. From a young age, Lewis had an interest in natural history. His mother taught him to collect and use medicinal plants. He also enjoyed hunting and being outdoors.

Lewis was well educated. He was interested in science. To prepare himself, Lewis learned about plants and animals. He studied medicine, too. Lewis secretly asked his friend, William Clark, to join him. Clark had been an army officer. He knew how to live in the wild. Clark was outgoing. He could draw maps and also knew how to build. Together, they made a great team.

Lewis and Clark found over 40 other men for the voyage. These men had special talents. Some were tailors, carpenters, and soldiers. Clark took his slave, York, with him. This group was known as the Corps of Discovery. If they made great discoveries, the United States would reward them. They set out on May 14, 1804, to explore the West.

Name: _____ Date: _____

Corps of Discovery (cont.)

Directions: Use the text to answer the questions below.

1 What is the main purpose of the text? Support your answer with evidence from the text.

_____

_____

_____

2 What is the author's point of view on the topic of the Louisiana Purchase in the text? Provide evidence from the text to support your answer.

_____

_____

_____

_____

3 How does the narrator's point of view influence the description of the events that occur in the story?

_____

_____

_____

4 What specific language does the author use to persuade the reader?

_____

_____

_____

_____

Excerpt from

The Heart of Darkness
by Joseph Conrad

The Nellie, a cruising yawl, swung to her anchor without a flutter of the sails, and was at rest. The wind was nearly calm, and being bound down the river, the only thing for it was to come to and wait for the turn of the tide.

The sea-reach of the Thames stretched before us like the beginning of an interminable waterway. In the offing the sea and the sky were welded together without a joint, and in the luminous space the tanned sails of the barges drifting up with the tide seemed to stand still in red clusters of canvas sharply peaked, with gleams of varnished sprits. A haze rested on the low shores that ran out to sea in vanishing flatness. The air was dark above Gravesend, and farther back still seemed condensed into a mournful gloom, brooding motionless over the biggest, and the greatest, town on earth.

The Director of Companies was our captain and our host. We four affectionately watched his back as he stood in the bows looking to seaward. On the whole river there was nothing that looked half so nautical. He resembled a pilot, which to a seaman is trustworthiness personified. It was difficult to realize his work was not out there in the luminous estuary, but behind him, within the brooding gloom.

Between us there was, as I have already said somewhere, the bond of the sea. Besides holding our hearts together through long periods of separation, it had the effect of making us tolerant of each other's yarns—and even convictions. The Lawyer—the best of old fellows—had, because of his many years and many virtues, the only cushion on deck, and was lying on the only rug. The Accountant had brought out already a box of dominoes, and was toying architecturally with the bones. Marlow sat cross-legged right aft, leaning against the mizzen-mast. He had sunken cheeks, a yellow complexion, a straight back, an ascetic aspect, and, with his arms dropped, the palms of hands outwards, resembled an idol. The Director, satisfied the anchor had good hold, made his way aft and sat down amongst us. We exchanged a few words lazily. Afterwards there was silence on board the yacht. For some reason or other we did not begin that game of dominoes. We felt meditative, and fit for nothing but placid staring. The day was ending in a serenity of still and exquisite brilliance. The water shone pacifically; the sky, without a speck, was a benign immensity of unstained light; the very mist on the Essex marshes was like a gauzy and radiant fabric, hung from the wooded rises inland, and draping the low shores in diaphanous folds. Only the gloom to the west, brooding over the upper reaches, became more somber every minute, as if angered by the approach of the sun.

And at last, in its curved and imperceptible fall, the sun sank low, and from glowing white changed to a dull red without rays and without heat, as if about to go out suddenly, stricken to death by the touch of that gloom brooding over a crowd of men.

#51449—TDQs: Strategies for Building Text-Dependent Questions

Name: _____ Date: _____

Excerpt from
The Heart of Darkness
by Joseph Conrad *(cont.)*

Directions: Use the text to answer the questions below.

1 Who is telling the story? How do you know?

_____

_____

_____

_____

2 What is the effect of the perspective of the narrator on the overall story? Support your answer with evidence from the text.

_____

_____

_____

_____

3 How does the author use point of view to convey emotion to the reader?

_____

_____

_____

_____

4 How does the narrator's point of view influence the description of the events that occur in the story?

_____

_____

_____

_____

Rotations in Geometry

When you go to an amusement park, do you enjoy riding the slow Ferris wheel? Or do you prefer fast, spinning rides that flip you upside down?

A **transformation** is the adjustment of a figure. The figure can be the same size and shape as the original, but it can be in a different position, or the figure can be stretched or shrunk. One type of transformation is the **rotation**, which can also be called a turn. When a figure is rotated, it is moved around a single, fixed point called the **center of rotation**. Imagine being on the Ferris wheel or the faster, spinning ride. In both cases, you become the figure being rotated around a single, fixed point in the center.

Rotational Symmetry

When an entire shape can be rotated with no change in its appearance, then that shape has **rotational symmetry**. Each figure below has rotational symmetry. Place your finger on the center of the first figure and turn the paper upside down. The resulting figure should look just like the original. You can try this with the second figure with 120° turns, the third figure with 90° turns, and the last figure with 72° turns.

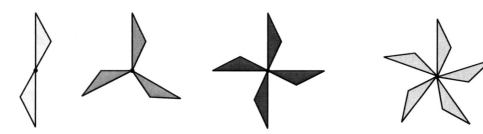

Rotations with Various Center Points

Key Details to Know

- The center of rotation may be anywhere in the plane—even on the figure itself.

- Turns can be measured with angle measurements. Phrases like "half-turn" may also be used. For example, if you turn the number 6 with a half-turn, you get the number 9.

- Rotations have direction. A turn may be clockwise ↻ or counterclockwise ↺.

- When a figure is rotated about a point, the turn may be described by the angle of rotation and by the direction.

Name: _____ Date: _____

Rotations in Geometry *(cont.)*

Directions: Use the text to answer the questions below.

1 What is the main purpose of the text? Support your answer with evidence from the text.

_____

_____

_____

_____

2 What does the author want the reader to understand through the text? Provide examples from the text to support your answer.

_____

_____

_____

_____

3 Does the author accomplish his/her purpose in the text? Provide examples and details from the text to support your opinion.

_____

_____

_____

_____

4 How do the style and content of the text contribute to the author's purpose?

_____

_____

_____

_____

Excerpt from
Frankenstein, or the Modern Prometheus
by Mary Wollstonecraft Shelley

To Mrs. Saville, England:

You will rejoice to hear that no disaster has accompanied the commencement of an enterprise which you have regarded with such evil forebodings. I arrived here yesterday, and my first task is to assure my dear sister of my welfare and increasing confidence in the success of my undertaking.

I am already far north of London, and as I walk in the streets of Petersburg, I feel a cold northern breeze play upon my cheeks, which braces my nerves and fills me with delight. Do you understand this feeling? This breeze, which has travelled from the regions towards which I am advancing, gives me a foretaste of those icy climes. Inspirited by this wind of promise, my daydreams become more fervent and vivid. I try in vain to be persuaded that the pole is the seat of frost and desolation; it ever presents itself to my imagination as the region of beauty and delight. There, Margaret, the sun is forever visible, its broad disk just skirting the horizon and diffusing a perpetual splendor. There—for with your leave, my sister, I will put some trust in preceding navigators—the snow and frost are banished; and, sailing over a calm sea, we may be wafted to a land surpassing in wonders and in beauty every region hitherto discovered on the habitable globe. What may not be expected in a country of eternal light? I may there discover the wondrous power which attracts the needle and may regulate a thousand celestial observations that require only this voyage to render their seeming eccentricities consistent forever. I shall satiate my ardent curiosity with the sight of a part of the world never before visited, and may tread a land never before imprinted by the foot of man. These are my enticements, and they are sufficient to conquer all fear of danger or death and to induce me to commence this laborious voyage with the joy a child feels when he embarks in a little boat, with his holiday mates, on an expedition of discovery up his native river. But supposing all these conjectures to be false, you cannot contest the inestimable benefit which I shall confer on all mankind, to the last generation, by discovering a passage near the pole to those countries, to reach which at present so many months are requisite; or by ascertaining the secret of the magnet, which, if at all possible, can only be effected by an undertaking such as mine.

These reflections have dispelled the agitation with which I began my letter, and I feel my heart glow with an enthusiasm, for nothing contributes so much to tranquillize the mind as a steady purpose—a point on which the soul may fix its intellectual eye. This expedition has been the favorite dream of my early years. I have read with ardor the accounts of the various voyages which have been made in the prospect of arriving at the North Pacific Ocean through the seas which surround the pole. My education was neglected, yet I was passionately fond of reading. My reading only increased the regret which I had felt, as a child, on learning that my father's dying injunction had forbidden my uncle to allow me to embark in a seafaring life.

Excerpt from
Frankenstein, or the Modern Prometheus
by Mary Wollstonecraft Shelley *(cont.)*

These visions faded when I perused, for the first time, those poets whose effusions entranced my soul and lifted it to heaven. I also became a poet and for one year lived in a paradise of my own creation; I imagined that I also might obtain a niche in the temple where the names of Homer and Shakespeare are consecrated. You are well acquainted with my failure and how heavily I bore the disappointment. But just at that time I inherited the fortune of my cousin, and my thoughts were turned into the channel of their earlier bent.

Six years have passed since I resolved on my present undertaking. I can, even now, remember the hour from which I dedicated myself to this great enterprise. I commenced by inuring my body to hardship. I accompanied the whale-fishers on several expeditions to the North Sea; I voluntarily endured cold, famine, thirst, and want of sleep; I often worked harder than the common sailors during the day and devoted my nights to the study of mathematics, the theory of medicine, and those branches of physical science from which a naval adventurer might derive the greatest practical advantage. And now, dear Margaret, do I not deserve to accomplish some great purpose? My life might have been passed in ease and luxury, but I preferred glory to every enticement that wealth placed in my path. Oh, that some encouraging voice would answer in the affirmative! My courage and my resolution is firm; but my hopes fluctuate, and my spirits are often depressed. I am about to proceed on a long and difficult voyage, the emergencies of which will demand all my fortitude: I am required not only to raise the spirits of others, but sometimes to sustain my own, when theirs are failing.

This is the most favorable period for travelling in Russia. They fly quickly over the snow in their sledges; the motion is pleasant, and, in my opinion, far more agreeable than that of an English stagecoach. The cold is not excessive, if you are wrapped in furs—a dress which I have already adopted, for there is a great difference between walking the deck and remaining seated motionless for hours, when no exercise prevents the blood from actually freezing in your veins. I have no ambition to lose my life on the post-road between St. Petersburg and Archangel. I shall depart for the latter town in a fortnight or three weeks; and my intention is to hire a ship there, which can easily be done by paying the insurance for the owner, and to engage as many sailors as I think necessary among those who are accustomed to the whale-fishing. I do not intend to sail until the month of June; and when shall I return? Ah, dear sister, how can I answer this question? If I succeed, many, many months, perhaps years, will pass before you and I may meet. If I fail, you will see me again soon, or never. Farewell, my dear, Margaret. Heaven shower down blessings on you, and save me, that I may again thank you for all your love and kindness.

Your affectionate brother,

R. Walton

Name: _____   Date: _____

Excerpt from
Frankenstein, or the Modern Prometheus
by Mary Wollstonecraft Shelley *(cont.)*

Directions: Use the text to answer the questions below.

1 Who is telling the story? How do you know?

_____

_____

_____

_____

2 How does the narrator's point of view differ from his sister's point of view? Support your answer with examples from the text.

_____

_____

_____

_____

3 What is the author's point of view on the topic of adventure and exploration in the text? Provide evidence from the text to support your answer.

_____

_____

_____

_____

4 How does the author use point of view to draw the reader into the story?

_____

_____

_____

_____

Excerpt from
Women and War Work
by Helen Fraser

What the War Has Done for Women

The war [World War I] already has done many great things for women in England. So many of these things are so naturally accepted now, that it is almost difficult to realize where we stood when the war broke out.

General Smuts said, "Under stress of great difficulty practically everything breaks down ultimately, and the only things that survive are really the simple human feelings of loyalty and comradeship to your fellows, and patriotism, which can stand any strain and bear you through all difficulty and privation. We soldiers know the extraordinary value of these simple feelings, how far they go and what strain they can bear, and how, ultimately, they support the whole weight of civilization."

In this war our men, in their dealings with us, have got down more and more to simple fundamental truths and facts—loyalty and comradeship, founded on our common patriotism. We have got nearer to the ideal so many of us long for, equal right to serve and help. The great fundamental establishment of political rights for women has come with us. When war broke out, women's suffrage was winning all the time a greater mass of adherents. A majority of the House was pledged to vote for it. The Trade Unions and Labour Party stood solidly for it, but the motive to act seemed lacking.

War came, and every political party in our country laid aside political agitation. No party meetings have been held since August, 1914. Suffragists and anti-suffragists did the same. The great body of suffragists kept their organization intact but used it for "sustaining the vital energies of the nation." The Suffrage societies flung themselves into relief and welfare work with ardor, zeal and ability. No women knew better how to organize, no women better how to educate and win help. They formed an admirable Women's Interests Committee, and looked after all women's interests excellently. When the Government issued its first appeal for women volunteers for munitions and land, etc., it asked the Suffrage societies to circulate them. These societies helped them to secure the needed labor from women.

As the war went on, it became clearer that the men of the country saw more vividly why suffragists had asked for vote. More and more men were impressed with the value of women's work. At meetings to do propaganda for Government appeals, women often spoke on the needs of the country. As a result, men everywhere, although it had nothing to do with the appeal, and had never been mentioned, declared their conversion to Women's Suffrage in the War.

Women pointed out that they did not want Women's Suffrage as a reward, but as a simple right. They had not worked for a reward, but for their country, as any citizen would. The Press came out practically solidly for Women's Suffrage. The work of women was praised in every paper. One declared, "It cannot be tolerable that we should return

Excerpt from
Women and War Work
by Helen Fraser (cont.)

to the old struggle about admitting them to the franchise." Eminent Anti-Suffragists frankly admitted their conversion. Mr. Asquith, the old enemy of Women's Suffrage, said in a memorable speech: "They presented to me not only a reasonable, but, I think, from their point of view, an unanswerable case.... They say that when the war comes to an end, and when the process of industrial reconstruction has to be set on foot, have not the women a special claim to be heard on the many questions which will arise directly affecting their interests, and possibly meaning for them large displacement of labor? I cannot think that the House will deny that, and, I say quite frankly, that I cannot deny that claim." It was clear the whole question of suffrage would need to be gone into. So after several attempts to deal with the problem in sections, a Committee was set up under the Speaker of the House of Commons to go into the whole question of Franchise reform and registration.

The Committee was composed of five Peers and twenty-seven members of the House of Commons, and started its work in October, 1916, and in its report, April, 1917, it recommended, by a majority, that a measure of enfranchisement should be given to women.

One thing is clear when considering the practical facts of new opportunities for women. Masses of our women took their new work as "temporary war workers." As the war has gone on, however, it has become clearer that many of these tasks are going to be permanently open to women. One reason is that many of the men will never return to take up their work again. Another, that many of them will never return to what they did before.

There is the other fact that we, like every other country, will need to repair and renovate so much. We will need to create more industries, increase our productiveness to pay off our burdens of debt, and to carry out our schemes of reconstruction. Women will still be needed to achieve these goals. Our women, in still greater numbers, will not be able to marry, and the best thing for any nation and any set of women is to do work. There will be plenty of room for all the work our women can do. Many will go back home to work, of course. There are large numbers who are working in our country only while their husbands are away. When the men return, these women will find their work in their homes again.

In special branches of work our opportunities are very much greater and better. Medicine is one of the professions in which women have very specially made good. Better training opportunities have opened and more funds have been raised to enable women of small means to get medical education. The Queen herself gave a portion of a gift of money she received for this purpose! Most medical appointments are open to women now and they have been urged by the great medical bodies to enter for training in the different Universities. Many women have followed this urging and have done so.

#51449—TDQs: Strategies for Building Text-Dependent Questions

Name: _____ Date: _____

Excerpt from
Women and War Work
by Helen Fraser *(cont.)*

Directions: Use the text to answer the questions below.

1 What is the author's point of view in the text? How do you know?

_____

_____

_____

_____

2 How is your point of view the same or different from the author's? Use textual evidence to justify your responses.

_____

_____

_____

_____

3 What language does the author use to advance her viewpoint? Is the use of this language effective? Use specific words and phrases from the text to justify your answer.

_____

_____

_____

_____

4 Does the author acknowledge others' points of view in the text? How so? Include examples from the text to support your answer.

_____

_____

_____

_____

#51449—TDQs: Strategies for Building Text-Dependent Questions

Analysis of Arguments and Claims

Text-dependent questions (TDQs) are important to the understanding of analysis of arguments and claims. In this section, you will find an overview, sample text-dependent questions/prompts, and informational passages, as well as supporting questions/prompts to use with your students. There are no literary texts included in this section because arguments and claims are only found within informational text. Below is a chart that provides the titles and the recommended grade ranges for the texts in this section.

Grade Range	Informational Text	Page #
K–1	*Bears*	226
2–3	Excerpt from *Amazing Americans: Susan B. Anthony* by Stephanie Kuligowski	228
4–5	*Life in Colonial America*	230
6–8	Excerpt from *Jane Goodall: Animal Scientist and Friend* by Connie Jankowski	233
9–12	Excerpt from *The Declaration of the United States of America*	235

Analysis of Arguments and Claims Overview

Within the realm of informational writing, one common use of written text is the expression of arguments or claims. Politicians communicate their worthiness and goals through convincing speeches, scientists secure funding and perform research to prove their hypotheses, and newspapers and magazines express authors' opinions through editorials. In this age of multimedia technology, savvy advertisers employ a myriad of marketing techniques to convince consumers to buy their products and popular bloggers debate the merits of everything from the newest gadgets to the latest educational trends. Due to the frequent presentation of arguments and claims in informational writing, it is particularly important that students have the skills to be able to recognize, comprehend, and analyze arguments and claims when they are reading informational text.

Under the category of reading, the eighth anchor standard in the Common Core states that students should be able to, "Delineate and evaluate the argument and specific claims in a text, including the validity of the reasoning as well as the relevance and sufficiency of the evidence" (2010). According to O'Reilly and Stooksbury (2013), "an argument/claim is supported by evidence that can be debated or challenged" while "an opinion is simply supported by more opinion" (105). In the Common Core, students start by learning how to identify the reasons authors give to support the points in the text. Eventually they learn how to be more specific in their analysis by understanding how specific reasons and evidence in the text support particular points. Next, students begin to evaluate arguments and claims by differentiating between those claims that are supported by evidence and those that are not. Ultimately, students need to be able to take their analysis even further by evaluating whether or not the evidence used to support the argument or claim is relevant and sufficient.

Text-dependent questions are an excellent tool for teaching students about arguments and claims in informational writing because they guide students back to the text in order to find the supporting textual evidence used to develop the claim or argument. Once they have identified the argument or claim and corresponding evidence used to support it, text-dependent questions then enable students to critically analyze each piece of evidence to see whether or not it truly corroborates the argument. Only after students understand all of the facets of the argument, and the individual reasons that support each facet, can they truly evaluate the validity of the claim in its entirety.

Text-Dependent Questions/Prompts

Arguments/Claims

- What is the author trying to tell the reader? What specific reasons does he/she give to support this point in the text?

- What is the author's main argument/claim in the text? How do you know?

- Why does the author claim _____ in the text? Support your answer with evidence from the text.

- What reasons/evidence does the author give to support the argument that _____ in the text?

- Describe how the author uses specific points to support the claim in the text. Include examples from the text in your answer.

- What specific reason(s) does the author give for claiming _____?

- How does the text structure support the author's reasons for his/her argument?

- What reasons does the author provide to support his/her claim that _____? Describe each reason.

- What is the connection between the sentence that starts with "_____" and the one that starts with "_____"? How do these two sentences support the author's main claim?

- How does the paragraph about _____ relate to the paragraph about _____? How do these two paragraphs work together to support the author's main claim?

- What evidence does the author provide to support the point that _____?

- What points in the text support the statement/claim that says, "_____"?

- Describe how the author develops the claim that _____. Include specific words and examples from the text.

- How does the author use constitutional principles to validate his/her argument/claim? Cite specific principles from the text in your answer.

- What legal reasoning does the author use to support his/her argument/claim in the text?

- What is the purpose of the text "_____"? How does the argument presented in this work play a role in history? Include evidence from the text to support your answer.

- What is the historical context of the claim presented in the text? How did the outcome of this argument/claim affect _____?

Text-Dependent Questions/Prompts (cont.)

Evaluation

- Evaluate the effectiveness of the author's claim. Support your opinion with examples from the text.

- Which claims in the text are supported by reasons? Which are not?

- Why is _____ a stronger claim than _____ in the text? Include evidence/examples from the text to support your answer.

- Does the author make any claims that are not supported by reasons or evidence? If so, which ones?

- Does the author use sound reasoning to support his/her claim that _____? Justify your answer with support from the text.

- Evaluate the evidence presented to support the argument that _____. Is the evidence relevant? Is it sufficient to support the author's claim?

- What problems do you see with the author's reasoning about his/her claim? How could you counter his/her reasoning? Include specific details from the text in your answer.

- Is the author's reasoning convincing? What parts of the text make it this way?

- Is the evidence presented to support the author's argument/claim relevant? Use examples from the text to explain why or why not.

- How does the author validate his/her claim in the text? Is this reasoning sufficient/enough? Be sure to refer back to the text in your answer.

- Do you trust the reasoning behind the author's argument/claim? What elements of the text make you feel this way?

- What emotions are evoked in the reader by the author's arguments/claims? How does this contribute to/support the effectiveness of the arguments/claims in the text? Use specific examples from the text to support your answer.

Bears

Bears are interesting. They eat many kinds of food. They live in many different places.

Polar bears live in the Arctic. They only eat meat. Seals are their favorite food. Polar bears like to swim. They can swim up to 100 miles.

Brown bears are the most common. They live in many countries around the world. They have strong shoulders. They are great diggers. They dig up tree roots for food. They dig out dens to sleep in. They also eat meat.

The giant panda bear lives in China. There are not many in the wild. Panda bears are shy. They only eat bamboo. They must eat a lot. They can weigh up to 300 pounds!

There are many types of bears. Each type is unique. These things make them interesting.

Name: _____ Date: _____

Bears (cont.)

Directions: Use the text to answer the questions below.

1 What is the author's main claim in the text? How do you know?

_____

_____

_____

_____

_____

_____

2 How does the author use specific points to support the claim in the text? Include examples from the text in your answer.

_____

_____

_____

_____

_____

_____

_____

Excerpt from
Amazing Americans: Susan B. Anthony
by Stephanie Kuligowski

Susan B. Anthony was an amazing American. She was a very smart woman. She also had a lot of courage. She believed all people are equal.

Susan was born on February 15th, 1820. She grew up in the state of Massachusetts. She was a bright child. She could read when she was three years old. She became a teacher when she grew up. She taught in New York. She earned $110 a year. Male teachers earned $400 a year. Susan thought this was unfair. She wanted better pay for women.

Susan wanted to change the world. She fought for women's rights. She also fought for the rights of African Americans. Susan wanted to change the way people were treated. Long ago, men had more rights than women. Women could not own a house. They could not vote. Susan wanted to change these ways. She wanted women to have the right to vote. This right was called suffrage.

People worked hard for suffrage. Susan and her friends marched in parades. They gave speeches. They also led meetings. They did not give up. They wanted equal rights for women.

Susan was an activist. She took action to make her world a better place. Susan saw the end of slavery during her life. She never got to vote legally though. She died in 1906. Women won the right to vote in the United States in 1920.

Name: _____ Date: _____

Excerpt from
Amazing Americans: Susan B. Anthony
by Stephanie Kuligowski *(cont.)*

Directions: Use the text to answer the questions below.

1 What specific reasons does the author give for claiming Susan B. Anthony was an amazing American?

_____

_____

_____

_____

2 Describe how the author develops the claim that Susan B. Anthony had a lot of courage. Include specific words and examples from the text.

_____

_____

_____

_____

3 Do you trust the reasoning behind the author's claim about Susan B. Anthony being an amazing American? What in the text makes you feel this way?

_____

_____

_____

_____

Life in Colonial America

Before the American Revolution, there were 13 British colonies in America. The people that lived in these colonies were called colonists. Colonists came from many countries. Some came from England. Others came from countries like Germany and Sweden. Some colonists came to claim land. Others hoped to find gold and get rich. Many colonists came to escape religious persecution. They wanted to be able to practice their religions freely.

Life as a colonist was very difficult. Most colonists had to endure long and challenging sea voyages to arrive in America. Many people died on the journey. Once they reached America, their hardships continued. Many colonists did not know how to survive in the wilderness. Some died from starvation. Others died from disease.

The colonists had to provide everything themselves. They built houses from brick and wood. Each house had a fireplace. The fireplace was made of brick. The fire gave light. It also kept the colonists warm. Some colonists used it for cooking, too. They also had to make all of their furniture from wood.

The colonists worked all year to provide food for their families. They hunted animals such as deer and rabbits. They ate the meat for food. They also preserved the meat for the long, cold winters. The colonists used the animal skins to make clothing. Colonial families also had gardens to grow vegetables. They kept cows and chickens for milk and eggs.

The colonists had to make their own clothing. They first had to make thread from plant fibers, such as cotton. Then, they wove the thread into cloth. Once they had cloth, they could cut and sew it to make clothes.

As more colonists arrived in America, they developed more specialized jobs. Some colonists were blacksmiths. They made tools from iron. Carpenters built houses and other structures. Coopers made buckets and barrels from wood. Cobblers made shoes from leather. Many colonists were farmers. They grew food for their families and sold extra food to other people. Everyone in the colonies worked very hard.

#51449—TDQs: Strategies for Building Text-Dependent Questions

Life in Colonial America *(cont.)*

Colonial children were expected to work hard, too. The girls helped with chores at home. They cooked, cleaned, and learned to sew. Boys often helped their fathers with work on the farm. They planted seeds and helped with the harvest. When they did have free time, the children played games like hide-and-seek and hopscotch.

Despite these difficult conditions, the early colonists survived. Through hard work and determination, they built new lives for themselves and their families in America.

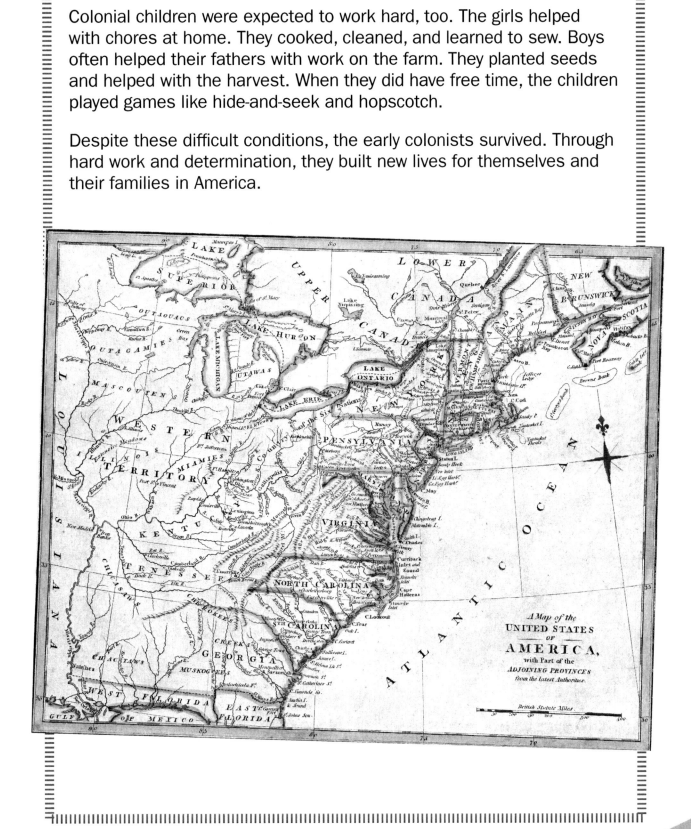

Name: _____ Date: _____

Life in Colonial America *(cont.)*

Directions: Use the text to answer the questions below.

1 What evidence does the author provide to support the point that life was difficult for the early colonists?

_____

_____

_____

2 How does the paragraph about housing relate to the paragraph about food? How do these two paragraphs work together to support the author's main claim?

_____

_____

_____

3 What points in the text support the statement that says, "Through hard work and determination, they built new lives for themselves and for their families in America"?

_____

_____

_____

4 Is the evidence presented to support the author's claim relevant? Use examples from the text to explain why or why not.

_____

_____

_____

Excerpt from

Jane Goodall: Animal Scientist and Friend
by Connie Jankowski

Goodall's Never-Ending Journey

Jane Goodall is an authority on chimpanzees. In fact, she is the world's leading authority. She once lived in a comfortable home, but then she left it all to live in the jungle. She gave up modern conveniences and lived in conditions that few would tolerate. She followed her heart and she found peace, friendship, and a world filled with fascinating creatures in Africa.

Goodall has devoted her life to learning about chimps. Her work has been in journals, books, and even on television shows. Her work is respected worldwide and she has become a model for others to follow.

Field Research

Goodall arrived in Tanzania in the summer of 1960, ready to study chimpanzees. The chimpanzees did not greet her warmly and they ran whenever they saw her. Goodall never gave up though. She kept her distance and watched through her binoculars.

Goodall tried to fit in with the group by keeping as quiet as possible. She learned to do things like the chimps and she knew to wait for the chimps to show they were ready. She didn't want to push herself on them and, eventually, her patience paid off. The chimps slowly accepted her and, little by little, they came closer and closer to Goodall.

After a few months, she watched two chimps strip leaves from a branch and then use the branch as a tool. They used it to pull termites out of a nest, showing that chimps are more intelligent than was thought before. Scientists thought using tools was something only humans could do, but Goodall proved them wrong.

Goodall saw a lot during her first year in the jungle. People thought chimps ate only insects and small rodents, but Goodall watched them hunt and eat bushpigs. She saw that chimps each have their own personalities, minds, and emotions. She watched the families and studied how they interacted. She wrote all about them, including their rivalries and bonds with others in the group.

Sadly, Goodall also saw a gruesome side of the chimpanzee world when a four-year war broke out in the jungle between two different groups of chimps. This is the first record of a long-term war outside of human battles. Members of the two chimpanzee groups fought and one defeated the other in the end. Through her research, we can see that chimps are so much like us!

Name: _____ Date: _____

Excerpt from
Jane Goodall: Animal Scientist and Friend
by Connie Jankowski *(cont.)*

Directions: Use the text to answer the questions below.

1 What evidence does the author give to support the argument that Goodall is the "world's leading authority" on chimps in the text?

_____

_____

_____

_____

2 Why does the author claim that "Goodall has devoted her life to learning about chimps" in the text? Support your answer with evidence from the text.

_____

_____

_____

_____

3 Explain the text structure the author uses to present the reasons for her argument.

_____

_____

_____

_____

4 Which claims in the text are supported by reasons? Which are not?

_____

_____

_____

_____

Excerpt from

The Declaration of Independence of the United States of America

When in the Course of human events, it becomes necessary for one people to dissolve the political bands which have connected them with another, and to assume, among the Powers of the earth, the separate and equal station to which the Laws of Nature and of Nature's God entitle them, a decent respect to the opinions of mankind requires that they should declare the causes which impel them to the separation.

We hold these truths to be self-evident, that all men are created equal, that they are endowed by their Creator with certain unalienable Rights, that among these are Life, Liberty, and the pursuit of Happiness. That to secure these rights, Governments are instituted among Men, deriving their just powers from the consent of the governed, That whenever any Form of Government becomes destructive of these ends, it is the Right of the People to alter or to abolish it, and to institute new Government, laying its foundation on such principles and organizing its powers in such form, as to them shall seem most likely to affect their Safety and Happiness. Prudence, indeed, will dictate that Governments long established should not be changed for light and transient causes; and accordingly all experience hath shown, that mankind are more disposed to suffer, while evils are sufferable, than to right themselves by abolishing the forms to which they are accustomed. But when a long train of abuses and usurpations, pursuing invariably the same Object evinces a design to reduce them under absolute Despotism, it is their right, it is their duty, to throw off such Government, and to provide new Guards for their future security. Such has been the patient sufferance of these Colonies; and such is now the necessity which constrains them to alter their former Systems of Government. The history of the present King of Great Britain is a history of repeated injuries and usurpations, all having in direct object the establishment of an absolute Tyranny over these States. To prove this, let Facts be submitted to a candid world.

He has refused his Assent to Laws, the most wholesome and necessary for the public good.

He has forbidden his Governors to pass Laws of immediate and pressing importance, unless suspended in their operation till his Assent should be obtained; and when so suspended, he has utterly neglected to attend to them.

He has refused to pass other Laws for the accommodation of large districts of people, unless those people would relinquish the right of Representation in the Legislature, a right inestimable to them and formidable to tyrants only.

He has called together legislative bodies at places unusual, uncomfortable, and distant from the depository of their Public Records, for the sole purpose of fatiguing them into compliance with his measures.

He has dissolved Representative Houses repeatedly, for opposing with manly firmness his invasions on the rights of the people.

He has refused for a long time, after such dissolutions, to cause others to be elected; whereby the Legislative Powers, incapable of Annihilation, have returned to the People at large for their exercise; the State remaining in the meantime exposed to all the dangers of invasion from without, and convulsions within.

Excerpt from

The Declaration of Independence of the United States of America (cont.)

He has endeavored to prevent the population of these States; for that purpose obstructing the Laws of Naturalization of Foreigners; refusing to pass others to encourage their migration hither, and raising the conditions of new Appropriations of Lands.

He has obstructed the Administration of Justice, by refusing his Assent to Laws for establishing Judiciary Powers.

He has made judges dependent on his Will alone, for the tenure of their offices, and the amount and payment of their salaries.

He has erected a multitude of New Offices, and sent hither swarms of Officers to harass our People, and eat out their substance.

He has kept among us, in times of peace, Standing Armies without the Consent of our legislatures.

He has affected to render the Military independent of and superior to the Civil Power.

He has combined with others to subject us to a jurisdiction foreign to our constitution, and unacknowledged by our laws; giving his Assent to their Acts of pretended legislation:

For quartering large bodies of armed troops among us:

For protecting them, by a mock Trial, from Punishment for any Murders which they should commit on the Inhabitants of these States:

For cutting off our Trade with all parts of the world:

For imposing taxes on us without our Consent:

For depriving us, in many cases, of the benefits of Trial by Jury…

…We, therefore, the Representatives of the United States of America, in General Congress, Assembled, appealing to the Supreme Judge of the world for the rectitude of our intentions, do, in the Name, and by the Authority of the good People of these Colonies, solemnly publish and declare, That these United Colonies are, and of Right ought to be Free and Independent States; that they are Absolved from all Allegiance to the British Crown, and that all political connection between them and the State of Great Britain, is and ought to be totally dissolved; and that as Free and Independent States, they have full Power to levy War, conclude Peace, contract Alliances, establish Commerce, and to do all other Acts and Things which Independent States may of right do. And for the support of this Declaration, with a firm reliance on the Protection of Divine Providence, we mutually pledge to each other our Lives, our Fortunes and our sacred Honor.

Name: _____ Date: _____

Excerpt from
The Declaration of Independence of the United States of America *(cont.)*

Directions: Use the text to answer the questions below.

1 Which claims in the text are supported by reasons? Which are not?

_____

_____

_____

_____

2 What is the historical context of the claim presented in the text? How did the outcome of this argument/claim affect United States history?

_____

_____

_____

_____

3 Evaluate the effectiveness of the author's claim. Give examples from the text.

_____

_____

_____

_____

4 What emotions are evoked in the reader by the author's arguments? How does this contribute to the effectiveness of the arguments/claims in the text? Use specific examples from the text to support your answer.

_____

_____

_____

_____

#51449—TDQs: Strategies for Building Text-Dependent Questions

Comparison of Multiple Texts

Text-dependent questions (TDQs) are important to the understanding of the comparison of multiple texts. In this section, you will find an overview, sample text-dependent questions/prompts, literary and informational passages, as well as supporting questions/prompts to use with your students. Below is a chart that provides the titles and the recommended grade ranges for the texts in this section.

Grade Range	Text Type	Title 1	Title 2	Pages
K–1	Informational	*Getting Around School!*	*Follow That Map!*	246, 247
2–3	Literary	*Little Red Riding-Hood from Old-time Stories, Fairy Tales and Myths Retold by Children* by E. Louise Smythe	*Little Red Riding Hood*	250, 253
4–5	Informational	Excerpt from *Investigating Storms* by by Debra J. Housel	Excerpt from *Inside the Water Cycle* by William B. Rice	256, 257
6–8	Literary	*"She Walks in Beauty"* by Lord Byron	*Romeo and Juliet,* Act II, Scene II	259, 260

Grade Range	Text Type	Title 1	Title 2	Title 3	Pages
9–12	Informational	The Emancipation Proclamation	Lincoln's Gettysburg Address	Excerpt from Lincoln's Second Inaugural Address	262, 264, 265

Comparison of Multiple Texts Overview

The ability to compare one thing to another is a natural human tendency. Infants and toddlers readily compare faces so they can identify their parents or caregivers, older children compare tastes and textures of various foods to determine their preferences, and adults make comparative decisions about where to live, what to buy, and how to organize schedules and routines. Despite this natural human inclination to make comparisons, however, students need instruction in order to fully utilize these skills in an academic setting. According to Silver (2010), research indicates that teaching students to engage in comparative thinking leads to important beneficial gains in student achievement (6). Within the realm of reading, this means teaching students the higher-level analytic skills necessary to be able to compare two or more texts on topics such as theme, setting, event sequence, and much more. The comparative analysis of multiple texts is a complex skill that necessitates instruction, guidance, and practice in order to master. This section shows how text-dependent questions can be used to help students develop their ability to think comparatively about multiple texts and create convincing arguments that communicate their findings.

The ability to compare multiple texts is the focus of the ninth reading anchor standard in the Common Core State Standards. It reads that students should be able to, "Analyze how two or more texts address similar themes or topics in order to build knowledge or to compare the approaches the authors take" (NGA and CCSSO 2010). For this standard, there are two separate expected outcomes. First, students must be able to *build knowledge* through the comparison of texts. This requires that students compile and integrate knowledge from multiple sources in order to gain a comprehensive understanding of a particular topic or theme. Secondly, this standard also necessitates that students *compare the approaches the authors take*. To do this, students must evaluate two sets of individual information in order to identify the similarities and differences in the authors' approaches.

For literature, the grade-specific standards start with comparisons of literary elements such as characters, theme, setting, etc. In the older grades, these comparisons advance to include the examination of similar themes across different cultures or text genres. The standards for informational writing begin by focusing on the comparison of important points and key details between two texts on the same topic. Later, students are required to integrate information from multiple sources, analyze how different authors portray the same event or topic, and identify conflicting information in various texts on the same topic.

The comparative analysis of multiple texts can be a broad and daunting task, but text-dependent questions offer an effective way to guide students through the development of these skills. Text-dependent questions can help students recognize the relevant sections of text, identify the key points and topics, analyze important literary elements, and integrate information.

Text-Dependent Questions/Prompts

General

- How are the texts the same? How are they different? Refer to specific examples in the text to support your answer.

- How does culture affect the two versions of the story/event _____?

- How do the texts deal with the topic of _____? What are the similarities and difference between the texts?

- Describe how the two texts tell the story of _____. List at least three similarities and three differences.

- What are the main differences between _____ and _____?

- What similarities and differences do you notice between the multiple books by _____? Include specific examples from the texts to support your answer.

- How does the genre of these texts affect the similarities and differences between them?

- How did the author draw on material from _____ in his/her text?

- In what ways did the author transform material from _____ when he/she integrated it into his/her text?

- Compare and contrast the illustrations/pictures/visual elements in the two texts.

- Do these texts have similar or different tones? Compare and contrast the tones using examples and specific details from the text.

- What similar themes do these texts share? Provide examples from each text to support your answer.

- Compare and contrast the treatment of the topic of _____ in the texts.

Literary Elements

- How are the characters in the texts similar? How are they different?

- What are some of the similarities and differences between the way _____ is portrayed/shown/explained in the two different versions of the story?

- What role does culture play in the way _____ is described in the _____ version of the story _____? Include examples from the story to support your answer.

- How are the adventures of _____ in the story _____ the same and/or different from the adventures of _____ in the story _____?

- Compare and contrast the experiences of _____ in the story _____ with the experiences of _____ in the story _____.

- How do the experiences of the character _____ differ in the two different versions of the story _____?

Text-Dependent Questions/Prompts (cont.)

- Compare and contrast the experiences of _____ in the _____ versions of the story.

- What are the physical similarities and differences between the characters _____ and _____?

- Compare _____'s emotional state with that of _____ in the story/poem/ drama _____.

- What role does _____ play in the text _____? How is his/her role the same or different in the other versions of the text?

- How is the sequence of events the same and/or different in the two versions of the story _____?

- Compare and contrast the plot sequences in the texts. Include specific examples from the texts in your answer.

- What similarities are there between the themes in _____ and _____?

- How does the setting differ between _____ and _____?

- In the series _____, what differences do you notice about the character _____ throughout the texts?

- How does culture affect the way in which the stories deal with the theme of _____? Include specific examples and details from the text to support your answer.

- Are these texts from the same time period? Genre? What evidence from the text allows you to know this?

- How does the time period of the texts affect the portrayal of the theme of _____?

- Compare and contrast the pattern of events in the stories _____ and _____. How do the different cultures behind these stories affect the way the authors created the patterns of events?

- How is the portrayal of the historical time period of _____ different in these two stories?

- Compare and contrast the way the location of _____ is represented in these two stories. Why did the author of _____ choose to represent it this way? Justify your answer using textual evidence.

- How did the author of _____ fictionalize the character _____? What elements of _____ are historically accurate according to _____?

- What historical elements are the same between the stories? Which are different?

- What additional piece of literature is mentioned within the text of _____? How does _____ draw on the themes/character types from this piece of literature?

- What is the purpose of the author's reference to _____ within the text? What similarities are there between these two texts?

Text-Dependent Questions/Prompts (cont.)

- How does the author interpret the work of _____ in a modern way in the text?

- How does the theme in _____ relate to the theme in the classic work _____? Include specific examples and details from the text to support your answer.

- What is the relationship between the characters in _____ and the classic work _____? Why did the author chose to draw on this particular work? Justify your answer with evidence from the text.

- What is the role of genre in the way that these texts approach the theme of _____? Use examples from the text to support your answer.

- How does the form of each text (e.g., story, poem, drama, etc.) affect the way a similar theme or topic is communicated to the reader?

- Which text format do you think is most effective at communicating the theme of _____ to the reader? Justify your answer with specific details and examples from the text.

Informational Text

- How are the descriptions of _____ similar? How are they different? Use examples from the text to support your answer.

- How are the important points in the _____ texts similar? How are they different? Use specific details from the texts in your answer.

- What are the key points from the first text? What additional information about the same topic did you learn from the additional text(s)?

- Are the details about _____ in the texts similar or different? Justify your answer by providing evidence from the texts.

- Write _____ sentences that integrate the information on _____ from both texts.

- Describe how the information about _____ from _____ supports the information on the same topic from _____.

- Demonstrate how to combine the information from both texts to make a more detailed explanation of _____.

- How does _____'s presentation/account of _____ compare to _____'s presentation/account of the same event? Use textual evidence to support your answer.

- How are the two descriptions of _____ the same? How are they different?

- Compare and contrast the text structure of _____ and _____. Explain how text structure affects the authors' presentations of material on the same topic.

- What information is emphasized in the text by _____? What information is emphasized in the text by _____? How do these differences in emphasis affect the overall presentation of the information?

Text-Dependent Questions/Prompts (cont.)

- How does _____ interpret the facts about _____? What is _____'s interpretation? How do these interpretations shape the presentation of the key information about _____?

- What conflicting evidence about _____ is presented in the texts?

- Where do the texts disagree on matters of fact? Where do they disagree on matters of interpretation? Include specific examples from the text in your answer.

- What is the common purpose between _____ and _____? How do you know?

- Compare and contrast the historical significance of _____ and _____. What themes do these texts have in common?

- What similar themes do these texts share? Provide examples from each text to support your answer.

- How does the purpose of the texts affect the way in which the authors present information about the topic of _____?

- What common goal is shared by _____ and _____? What evidence from the text tells you this?

Getting Around School

How do you get from one place to another? A map can show you the way. This map shows a school. It uses shapes and lines. It also uses symbols. The symbols represent things. This map has symbols for the bathrooms. One is for boys. One is for girls. This map also shows three classrooms. It shows two offices. The light gray rectangle is the playground. The map tells you where these things are located. Maps are useful. They help you get around.

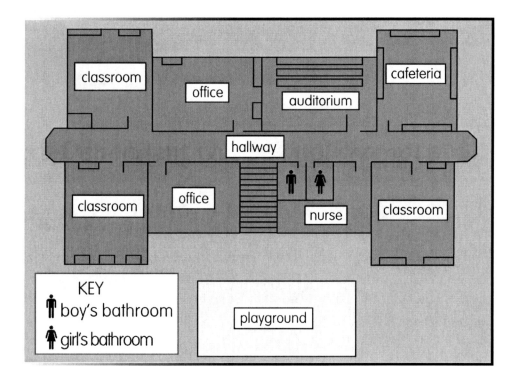

Follow That Map!

It is a party. We play games. We have a treasure hunt. We follow a map. We run to the first place on the map and look for treasure. The treasure is not there. We run to the second place. We look for treasure, but the treasure is not there either. We run to the third place and look for treasure. The treasure is here! We used the map. It gave us directions. We found the treasure!

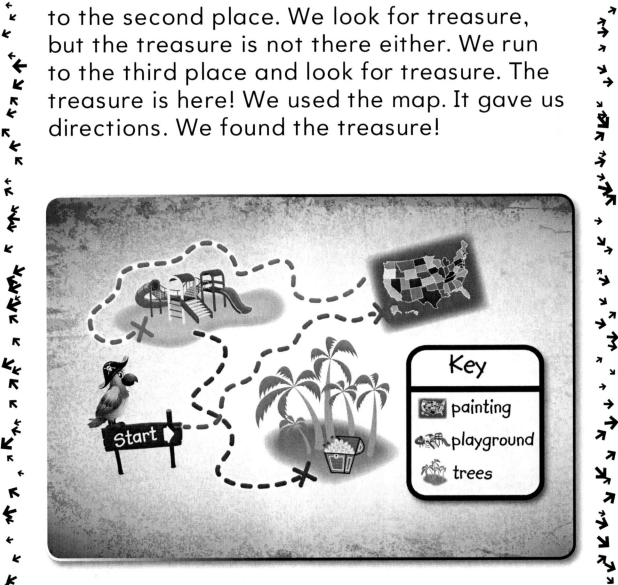

Name: _____ Date: _____

Using Maps Questions

Directions: Use the text to answer the questions below.

1 How are the descriptions of maps the same? How are they different? Use examples from the texts in your answer.

_____

_____

_____

_____

_____

2 What are the key points from the first text? What other information about the same topic did you learn from the second text?

_____

_____

_____

_____

_____

Name: _____ Date: _____

Using Maps Questions *(cont.)*

3 Are the details about maps in the texts similar or different? Use examples from the texts in your answer.

_____

- - - - - - - - - - - - - - - -

_____

_____

- - - - - - - - - - - - - - - -

_____

_____

- - - - - - - - - - - - - - - -

_____

4 Compare and contrast the pictures of maps in the two texts.

_____

- - - - - - - - - - - - - - - -

_____

_____

- - - - - - - - - - - - - - - -

_____

_____

- - - - - - - - - - - - - - - -

_____

Little Red Riding-Hood from Old-time Stories, Fairy Tales and Myths Retold by Children
by E. Louise Smythe

When May was six years old, her grandma made her a red coat with a hood. She looked so pretty in it that the children all called her "Red Riding-Hood."

One day her mama said, "I want you to take this cake and some butter to grandma." Red Riding-Hood was very glad to go. She always had a good time at grandma's house. She put the things into her little basket and ran off. When Red Riding-Hood came to the wood, she met a big wolf.

"Where are you going?" said the wolf.

Red Riding-Hood said, "I am going to see my grandma. Mama has made her a cake and butter."

"Does she live far?" said the wolf.

"Yes," said Red Riding-Hood, "in the white house by the mill."

"I will go too, and we shall see who will get there first," said the wolf.

The wolf ran off and took a short way, but Red Riding-Hood stopped to pick some flowers.

When the wolf got to the house, he tapped on the door. The grandma said, "Who is there?" The wolf made his voice as soft as he could.

#51449—TDQs: Strategies for Building Text-Dependent Questions

Little Red Riding-Hood from *Old-time Stories, Fairy Tales and Myths Retold by Children*
by E. Louise Smythe *(cont.)*

He said, "It is little Red Riding-Hood, Grandma."

Then the old lady said, "Pull the string and the door will open."

The wolf ran in and ate the poor old lady. Then he jumped into her bed and put on her cap.

When Red Riding-Hood tapped on the door, the wolf called out, "Who is there?" Red Riding-Hood said, "It is your little Red Riding-Hood, Grandma."

Then the wolf said, "Pull the string and the door will open."

When she went in, she said, "Look, Grandma, see the cake and butter mama has sent you."

"Thank you, dear, put them on the table and come here."

When Red Riding-Hood went near the bed, she said, "Oh, Grandma, how big your arms are!"

"The better to hug you, my dear."

"How big your ears are, Grandma."

"The better to hear you, my dear."

"How big your eyes are, Grandma."

Little Red Riding-Hood from *Old-time Stories, Fairy Tales and Myths Retold by Children*
by E. Louise Smythe *(cont.)*

"The better to see you, my dear."

"How big your teeth are, Grandma!"

"The better to eat you."

Then the cruel wolf jumped up and ate poor little Red Riding-Hood. Just then a hunter came by. He heard Red Riding-Hood shout. The hunter ran into the house and killed the old wolf. When he cut the wolf open, out jumped Little Red Riding-Hood and her grandma.

#51449—*TDQs: Strategies for Building Text-Dependent Questions* © *Shell Education*

Little Red Riding Hood

Once upon a time, there was a little girl called Little Red Riding Hood. One day, her mother asked Little Red Riding Hood to bring a basket of cookies to her grandmother. The girl's grandmother lived in the forest nearby. Little Red Riding Hood's mother told her to go straight to Grandmother's house. She told her to be very careful. Little Red Riding Hood took the basket of cookies and started off.

Soon, Little Red Riding Hood met a wolf in the forest.

"Where are you going?" asked the wolf.

"I'm bringing cookies to my grandmother," replied Little Red Riding Hood. "She lives in the forest by the mill."

"Why don't you bring your grandmother some flowers too?" said the wolf. "There are many pretty flowers."

Little Red Riding-Hood began to gather flowers. The wolf ran to Grandmother's house. When Grandmother saw the wolf, she was scared. She quickly hid under the bed. The wolf put on Grandmother's nightcap. He climbed into her bed to wait for Little Red Riding Hood.

When Little Red Riding-Hood arrived, she knocked on the door.

"Who is it?" called the wolf in a high-pitched voice.

Little Red Riding Hood (cont.)

"It is me, Little Red Riding Hood," said the girl. "I have brought you cookies from Mother."

"Come in," replied the wolf. "It is lovely to see you, my dear."

Little Red Riding Hood went to give her grandmother a hug. She said, "Oh, Grandma, how big your arms are!"

"The better to hug you, my dear."

"How big your ears are, Grandma."

"The better to hear you, my dear."

"How big your eyes are, Grandma."

"The better to see you, my dear."

"How big your teeth are, Grandma!"

"The better to eat you!" cried the wolf, jumping out of bed. He started chasing Little Red Riding Hood. Just then, a hunter happened to be walking by. He heard a scream from the house. He looked in the window to investigate. When he saw the wolf, he shot his gun into the air. The gunshot scared the wolf. He fled out the door, never to be seen again. Then, Grandmother came out from under the bed. She hugged Little Red Riding Hood and thanked the hunter. Then, they all sat down to enjoy tea and cookies together.

Name: _____ Date: _____

Little Red Riding Hood Questions

Directions: Use the text to answer the questions below.

1 How are the texts the same? How are they different? Use specific examples in the text to support your answer.

_____

_____

_____

_____

2 Compare and contrast the plot of *Little Red Riding Hood* in the two versions of the story.

_____

_____

_____

_____

3 What role does the hunter play in the text *Little Red Riding Hood*? How is his role the same or different in the two versions of the text?

_____

_____

_____

_____

Excerpt from
Investigating Storms
by Debra J. Housel

You're looking forward to a weekend full of sunshine so you check the news just to be sure the skies will be clear. The weather report says a storm is on the way. How do they know? The skies look clear and sunny. How can they tell that rain is coming?

Rain is a kind of **precipitation**. Precipitation is any form of water falling from the sky. It can be frozen like snow or liquid like rain. First, the water has to get into the air and then, something has to make it come down again. What happens to make it rain?

The sun heats the water on Earth's surface and this makes water **evaporate** from lakes, rivers, oceans, and the ground. The heated water turns into vapor, or a gas, and rises into the air and cools. It **condenses** and forms clouds and, eventually, some of the cloud drops get so big and heavy that they fall back to the earth. They come as rain, snow, sleet, freezing rain, or hail.

Raindrops are small groups of water molecules and dust. When they get too heavy to stay inside a cloud, they fall. When it's really cold, raindrops can freeze and become sleet, or they can become ice crystals. These crystals attach together to become snowflakes. When water vapor strikes a freezing surface, it looks like snow, but it has a special name. It is called frost.

No matter the name, water from the sky is always called the same thing, precipitation.

Freezing rain falls just as rain and then enters colder air. It's not in the cold air long enough to freeze though, it just becomes super cooled, almost to freezing. Then, the raindrops freeze as soon as they touch a surface.

Sometimes, raindrops freeze into chunks called hail. This happens when raindrops get caught in a cloud's updraft, or a stream of air that moves upward. When this happens, the raindrops become large ice pellets.

Wind is also a part of storms. Wind is moving air. Air is heavy and it pushes down on the ground beneath it, creating pressure. Wind is air that blows from high-pressure area to a low-pressure area. The greater the difference in air pressure, the faster the wind moves. This air pressure is measured with a **barometer**.

#51449—*TDQs: Strategies for Building Text-Dependent Questions* © *Shell Education*

Excerpt from
Inside the Water Cycle
by William B. Rice

Down Came the Rain

Rain has been falling hard for hours, but now it's starting to slow. Bit by bit, the drum of rain on the windowpane lessens. It becomes a soft drizzle until finally, a single drop strikes. Slowly it glides down the glass. At the end, it stops for a minute and then, plop! It drops to a puddle on the ground.

The sky is still covered in clouds, but the puddle slowly disappears. The water sinks into the soil, leaving mud behind and, when the sun comes out, the mud disappears. There is no sign of the water, and no sign of the rain that poured for hours. It seems like the water just never existed, but it did, and it still does. It exists in other forms and other places. It is somewhere within the **water cycle**.

'Round and 'Round We Go

The seasons, the days of the week, and the circle of life all have one thing in common. They are cycles. They move from one phase to another and then back to the beginning. Cycles follow the path from one place to another and back around again.

The truth is that cycles don't really have a start or finish; they just keep going like a circle. A circle has no start or end and the same is true for the water cycle because water moves from one phase to the next.

But water is just water—isn't it? How can it have phases? Water is **compound** which means that it is made of more than one **element**, or a naturally occurring substance. The elements that make water are hydrogen and oxygen.

Two hydrogen **atoms** combine with one oxygen atom to make one tiny **molecule** of water. This is written as H_2O. Billions of water molecules combine to make the liquid substance you know of as water.

H_2O doesn't have to be just a liquid. It can also be as solid as ice or it can be a gas as steam or vapor. No matter what, it's still water. It just changes form as it moves through the water cycle.

Name: _____ Date: _____

Water Cycle Questions

Directions: Use the text to answer the questions below.

1 How are the important points in the two texts similar? How are they different? Use specific details from the texts in your answer.

_____

_____

_____

_____

2 What is the common purpose between the two texts? How do you know?

_____

_____

_____

3 Are the details about water in the texts similar or different? Justify your answer by providing evidence from the texts.

_____

_____

_____

_____

4 How are the descriptions of precipitation similar? How are they different? Use examples from the text to support your answer.

_____

_____

_____

_____

"She Walks in Beauty"

from The Works of Lord Byron, Volume III
by Lord Byron

She walks in Beauty, like the night

Of cloudless climes and starry skies;

And all that's best of dark and bright

Meet in her aspect and her eyes:

Thus mellowed to that tender light

Which Heaven to gaudy day denies.

One shade the more, one ray the less,

Had half impaired the nameless grace

Which waves in every raven tress,

Or softly lightens o'er her face;

Where thoughts serenely sweet express,

How pure, how dear their dwelling-place.

And on that cheek, and o'er that brow,

So soft, so calm, yet eloquent,

The smiles that win, the tints that glow,

But tell of days in goodness spent,

A mind at peace with all below,

A heart whose love is innocent!

Romeo and Juliet, Act II, Scene II
Excerpt from *Leveled Texts for Classic Fiction: Shakespeare*

Romeo: But wait, what is that beautiful light coming from that window above me? Oh, it is the lovely Juliet, whose beauty radiates with the brightness of the sun, making the black sky and silver moon bothered and jealous because they know that Juliet's beaming beauty will always outshine their own weak light. When Juliet comes into a place, her sparking light makes everything around her look sickly, pale, and dull. From this moment on, Juliet is my lady and for eternity, Juliet is my love. I long to speak aloud to her about the passionate love I have for her, but instead, I am forced to hide here in the shadows beneath her window. I love every single and individual part of her and would find happiness in any part Juliet would be willing to bestow on me. If her eyes were the only thing that would notice me, I would be filled with joy for the simple fact that her eyes would look at me. Wait, she is speaking, but unfortunately, she is not speaking to me. Her eyes are perfect, glowing stars lighting the dark night, and the sky weeps with sorrow for the two missing stars that have left the gloom of night to shimmer brilliantly in Juliet's face. It is a face so glorious and light that it almost turns the murky dark of the night into the clear and visible light of day. I think I can hear the birds that see the light of Juliet's eyes and, believing she is the sun, they awake to sing their morning song in confusion. And look how she gently rests that breathtaking face in her soft hands. I long to be a glove on those hands, and I long to be allowed to caress that lovely face.

Juliet: Oh my!

Romeo: Juliet speaks; speak to me, lovely Juliet. You are the most magnificent thing I have ever seen, a white angel who has floated from the heavens to bring light and love to my sorry life.

Juliet: Romeo, oh Romeo! Why are you named Romeo? Can you break away from your name, Romeo? If you will release yourself from your name, I would be yours forever, but if it is impossible for you to leave your name, Romeo, I will give up mine. Tell me you love me, and I will never again be called Juliet Capulet.

Romeo: [Aside] Should I stay and hear what she has to say, or should I have the courage to speak to her now as she confesses her love for me?

Juliet: Romeo, it is not you that my family despises, but it is your name that is my enemy. Your name alone is the barrier between our love: Romeo Montague. But how can a name inspire hatred when you are so much more than just a name? Romeo is made up of so many different parts, like hands and arms and legs, but which one of those individual parts is your name? How can your name be the only thing that determines who you are? When I smell a rose, it smells sweet regardless of the name that I give it. Romeo, you are like that rose because even if I call you something else, you will still be the young man who has my love and my heart.

Name: _____ Date: _____

"She Walks in Beauty" and *Romeo and Juliet* Questions

Directions: Use the text to answer the questions below.

1 How are the texts the same? How are they different? Make sure to refer to specific examples in the text to support your answer.

_____

_____

_____

_____

2 How are the characters in the texts similar? How are they different?

_____

_____

_____

_____

3 Compare Romeo's emotional state with that of the narrator in the poem "She Walks in Beauty." Use examples from the text to support your answer.

_____

_____

_____

_____

4 Which text format do you think is most effective at communicating the theme of love or beauty to the reader? Justify your answer with specific details and examples from the text.

_____

_____

_____

_____

The Emancipation Proclamation
given by President Abraham Lincoln on September 22, 1862

Whereas on the 22nd day of September, A.D. 1862, a proclamation was issued by the President of the United States, containing, among other things, the following, to wit:

"That on the 1st day of January, A.D. 1863, all persons held as slaves within any State or designated part of a State the people whereof shall then be in rebellion against the United States shall be then, thenceforward, and forever free; and the executive government of the United States, including the military and naval authority thereof, will recognize and maintain the freedom of such persons and will do no act or acts to repress such persons, or any of them, in any efforts they may make for their actual freedom"?

"That the executive will on the 1st day of January aforesaid, by proclamation, designate the States and parts of States, if any, in which the people thereof, respectively, shall then be in rebellion against the United States; and the fact that any State or the people thereof shall on that day be in good faith represented in the Congress of the United States by members chosen thereto at elections wherein a majority of the qualified voters of such States shall have participated shall, in the absence of strong countervailing testimony, be deemed conclusive evidence that such State and the people thereof are not then in rebellion against the United States."

Now, therefore, I, Abraham Lincoln, President of the United States, by virtue of the power in me vested as Commander-In-Chief of the Army and Navy of the United States in time of actual armed rebellion against the authority and government of the United States, and as a fit and necessary war measure for suppressing said rebellion, do, on this 1st day of January, A.D. 1863, and in accordance with my purpose so to do, publicly proclaimed for the full period of one hundred days from the first day above mentioned, order and designate as the States and parts of States wherein the people thereof, respectively, are this day in rebellion against the United States the following, to wit:

Arkansas, Texas, Louisiana (except the parishes of St. Bernard, Palquemines, Jefferson, St. John, St. Charles, St. James, Ascension, Assumption, Terrebone, Lafourche, St. Mary, St. Martin, and Orleans, including the city of New Orleans), Mississippi, Alabama, Florida, Georgia, South Carolina, North Carolina, and Virginia (except the forty-eight counties designated as West Virginia, and also the counties of Berkeley, Accomac, Northhampton, Elizabeth City, York, Princess Anne, and Norfolk, including the cities of Norfolk and Portsmouth), and which excepted parts are for the present left precisely as if this proclamation were not issued.

The Emancipation Proclamation
given by President Abraham Lincoln on September 22, 1862 (cont.)

And by virtue of the power and for the purpose aforesaid, I do order and declare that all persons held as slaves within said designated States and parts of States are, and henceforward shall be, free; and that the Executive Government of the United States, including the military and naval authorities thereof, will recognize and maintain the freedom of said persons.

And I hereby enjoin upon the people so declared to be free to abstain from all violence, unless in necessary self-defense; and I recommend to them that, in all case when allowed, they labor faithfully for reasonable wages. And I further declare and make known that such persons of suitable condition will be received into the armed service of the United States to garrison forts, positions, stations, and other places, and to man vessels of all sorts in said service.

And upon this act, sincerely believed to be an act of justice, warranted by the Constitution upon military necessity, I invoke the considerate judgment of mankind and the gracious favor of Almighty God.

Lincoln's *Gettysburg Address*

given on November 19, 1863

Four score and seven years ago, our fathers brought forth upon this continent a new nation: conceived in liberty, and dedicated to the proposition that all men are created equal.

Now we are engaged in a great civil war ... testing whether that nation, or any nation so conceived and so dedicated ... can long endure. We are met on a great battlefield of that war.

We have come to dedicate a portion of that field as a final resting place for those who here gave their lives that this nation might live. It is altogether fitting and proper that we should do this.

But, in a larger sense, we cannot dedicate ... we cannot consecrate ... we cannot hallow this ground. The brave men, living and dead, who struggled here have consecrated it, far above our poor power to add or detract. The world will little note, nor long remember, what we say here, but it can never forget what they did here.

It is for us the living, rather, to be dedicated here to the unfinished work which they who fought here have thus far so nobly advanced. It is rather for us to be here dedicated to the great task remaining before us ... that from these honored dead we take increased devotion to that cause for which they gave the last full measure of devotion ... that we here highly resolve that these dead shall not have died in vain ... that this nation, under God, shall have a new birth of freedom ... and that government of the people ... by the people ... for the people ... shall not perish from this earth.

#51449—TDQs: Strategies for Building Text-Dependent Questions

Excerpt from
Lincoln's *Second Inaugural Address*
given on March 4, 1865

...On the occasion corresponding to this four years ago, all thoughts were anxiously directed to an impending civil war. All dreaded it—all sought to avert it. While the inaugural address was being delivered from this place, devoted altogether to saving the Union without war, insurgent agents were in the city seeking to destroy it without war—seeking to dissolve the Union, and divide effects, by negotiation. Both parties deprecated war; but one of them would make war rather than let the nation survive; and the other would accept war rather than let it perish. And the war came.

One-eighth of the whole population were colored slaves, not distributed generally over the Union, but localized in the Southern part of it. These slaves constituted a peculiar and powerful interest. All knew that this interest was, somehow, the cause of the war. To strengthen, perpetuate, and extend this interest was the object for which the insurgents would rend the Union, even by war; while the government claimed no right to do more than to restrict the territorial enlargement of it.

Neither party expected for the war the magnitude or the duration which it has already attained. Neither anticipated that the cause of the conflict might cease with, or even before, the conflict itself should cease. Each looked for an easier triumph, and a result less fundamental and astounding. Both read the same Bible, and pray to the same God; and each invokes his aid against the other. It may seem strange that any men should dare to ask a just God's assistance in wringing their bread from the sweat of other men's faces; but let us judge not, that we be not judged. The prayers of both could not be answered—that of neither has been answered fully...

...Fondly do we hope—fervently do we pray—that this mighty scourge of war may speedily pass away. Yet, if God wills that it continue until all the wealth piled by the bondsman's two hundred and fifty years of unrequited toil shall be sunk, and until every drop of blood drawn by the lash shall be paid by another drawn with the sword, as was said three thousand years ago, so still it must be said, "The judgments of the Lord are true and righteous altogether."

With malice toward none; with charity for all; with firmness in the right, as God gives us to see the right, let us strive on to finish the work we are in; to bind up the nation's wounds; to care for him who shall have borne the battle, and for his widow, and his orphan—to do all which may achieve and cherish a just and lasting peace among ourselves, and with all nations.

Name: _____ Date: _____

Lincoln Speech Questions

Directions: Use the text to answer the questions below.

1 What are the key points from the first text? What additional information about the same topic did you learn from the additional text(s)?

_____

_____

_____

_____

_____

2 Do these texts have similar or different tones? Compare and contrast the tones using examples and specific details from the text.

_____

_____

_____

_____

_____

3 How does the purpose of the texts affect the way in which the author presents information about the abolition of slavery?

_____

_____

_____

_____

_____

4 Compare and contrast the treatment of the topic of war in the texts.

_____

_____

_____

_____

References Cited

Bintz, William P., Petra Peinkosky Moran, Rochelle Berndt, Elizabath Ritz, Julie A. Skilton, and Lisa S. Bircher. 2012. "Using Literature to Teach Inference Across the Curriculum." *Voices from the Middle* 20: 16-24.

Brown, Sheila, and Lee Kappes. 2012. *Implementing the Common Core State Standards: A Primer on "Close Reading of Text."* Washington D.C.: The Aspen Institute.

Day, Richard R., and Jeong-suk Park. 2005. "Developing Reading Comprehension Questions." *Reading in Foreign Language* 17: 60-73.

Fisher, Douglas, and Nancy Frey. 2012. *Engaging the Adolescent Learner: Text-Dependent Questions*. International Reading Association.

Fisher, Douglas, Nancy Frey, and Cristina Alfaro. 2013. *The Path to Get There: A Common Core Road Map for Higher Student Achievement Across the Disciplines*. New York: Teachers College Press.

Fusco, Esther. 2012. *Effective Questioning Strategies in the Classroom: A Step-by-Step Approach to Engaged Thinking and Learning, K-8*. New York: Teachers College Press.

Ibe, Helen Ngozi. 2009. "Metacognitive Strategies on Classroom Participation and Student Achievement in Senior Secondary Science Classrooms." *Science Education International* 20: 25-31.

Kim, Youb. 2010. "Scaffolding Through Questions in Upper Elementary ELL Learning." *Literacy Teaching and Learning* 15: 109-136.

Kispal, Anne. 2008. *Effective Teaching of Inference Skills for Reading: Literature Review*. London, England: National Foundation for Educational Research.

Maria, Katherine. 1990. *Reading Comprehension Instruction: Issues and Strategies*. Parkton, MD: York Press.

McLaughlin, Maureen, and Brenda J. Overturf. 2013. *The Common Core: Teaching Students in Grades 6-12 to Meet the Reading Standards*. Newark, DE: International Reading Association.

McTighe, Jay, and Grant Wiggins. 2013. *Essential Questions: Opening Doors to Student Understanding*. Alexandria, VA: ASCD.

National Governors Association Center for Best Practices, Council of Chief State School Officers. 2010. *Common Core Standards*.

Nelson-Royes, Andrea. 2013. *Success in School and Career: Common Core Standards in Language Arts K–5*. Lanham, MD: Rowman and Littlefield Education.

O'Reilly, Stacey, and Angie Stooksbury. 2013. *Common Core Reading Lessons: Pairing Literary and Nonfiction Texts to Promote Deeper Understanding*. New York: Routledge.

Pasch, Grete, and Kent Norsworthy. 2001. *Using Internet Primary Sources to Teach Critical Thinking Skills in World Languages*. Westport, CT: Greenwood Press.

Silver, Harvey F. 2010. *Compare and Contrast: Teaching Comparative Thinking to Strengthen Student Learning*. Alexandria, VA: ASCD.

Contents of Digital Resource CD

Page	Title	Filename
24	*The Storm*	storm.pdf storm.doc
26	*The Brain*	brain.pdf brain.doc
28	*Why the Woodpecker Bores for Its Food*	woodpecker.pdf woodpecker.doc
32	*Our Earth*	earth.pdf earth.doc
35	Excerpt from *The Wind in the Willows* by Kenneth Grahame	windwillows.pdf windwillows.doc
38	*The World of Animals*	worldanimals.pdf worldanimals.doc
41	Excerpt from *The Rover Boys at School* by Edward Stratemeyer	roverboys.pdf roverboys.doc
44	*James Madison: Architect of the Constitution*	jamesmadison.pdf jamesmadison.doc
46	Excerpt from Chapter 1, *King Arthur and His Knights* by Sir James Knowles	kingarthur.pdf kingarthur.doc
50	Excerpt from *Origin and Development of Form and Ornament in Ceramic Art* by William H. Holmes	originform.pdf originform.doc
61	*Friends*	friends.pdf friends.doc
63	*Deserts*	deserts.pdf deserts.doc
65	"My Treasures" from *Child's Garden of Verses* by Robert Louis Stevenson	mytreasure.pdf mytreasure.doc
67	*Measuring the Length of Objects*	measuringlength.pdf measuringlength.doc
70	"The Wise Monkey and the Boar" from *Japanese Fairy Tales* compiled by Yei Theodora Ozaki	wisemonkey.pdf wisemonkey.doc
74	Excerpt from *Max Planck: Uncovering the World of Matter* by Jane Weir	maxplanck.pdf maxplanck.doc
77	Excerpt from *Hamlet*, Act IV, Scene VII by William Shakespeare	hamlet.pdf hamlet.doc

Contents of Digital Resource CD *(cont.)*

Page	Title	Filename
80	*World War II*	worldwar.pdf worldwar.doc
83	Excerpt from *The Scarlet Letter* by Nathaniel Hawthorne	scarletletter.pdf scarletletter.doc
86	*What Are Cells?*	cells.pdf cells.doc
95	*The Picky Boy*	pickyboy.pdf pickyboy.doc
97	*Your Sense of Taste*	taste.pdf taste.doc
99	"The Shoemaker and the Elves" from *The Beacon Second Reader* by James H. Fassett	shoemaker.pdf shoemaker.doc
102	Excerpt from *Solids* by Lisa Greathouse	solids.pdf solids.doc
105	Excerpt from *The Jungle Book* by Rudyard Kipling	junglebook.pdf junglebook.doc
108	*Collecting Data*	collectingdata.pdf collectingdata.doc
111	Excerpt from *Call of the Wild* by Jack London	callofwild.pdf callofwild.doc
113	Excerpt from *Ancient Rome* by Betsey Norris	ancientrome.pdf ancientrome.doc
115	Excerpt from Chapter 3, *Pride and Prejudice* by Jane Austen	pride.pdf pride.doc
118	Excerpt from *The Every-day Life of Abraham Lincoln* by Frances Fisher Browne	everydaylincoln.pdf everydaylincoln.doc
128	*Fritz*	fritz.pdf fritz.doc
130	*Frogs*	frogs.pdf frogs.doc
132	*The Three Little Pigs* from *English Fairy Tales* by Anonymous, Collected by Joseph Jacobs	littlepigsfairytales.pdf littlepigsfairytales.doc
135	*Earth's Layers*	earthlayers.pdf earthlayers.doc

Contents of Digital Resource CD (cont.)

Page	Title	Filename
138	*The Emperor's New Clothes* from *Andersen's Fairy Tales* by Hans Christian Andersen	newclothes.pdf newclothes.doc
141	*Being Sick*	beingsick.pdf beingsick.doc
144	Excerpt from Chapter 1, *A Little Princess* by Frances Hodgson Burnett	littleprincess.pdf littleprincess.doc
146	*Irish Immigration*	irishimmigration.pdf irishimmigration.doc
148	*The Bravery of Regulus* by Charlotte M. Yonge	braveryregulus.pdf braveryregulus.doc
151	Excerpt from Chapter 1, *Beethoven* by George Alexander Fischer	beethoven.pdf beethoven.doc
163	*My Pets*	pets.pdf pets.doc
165	*Whales*	whales.pdf whales.doc
167	Excerpt from *Peter Rabbit* by Beatrix Potter	peterrabbit.pdf peterrabbit.doc
170	*Understanding Place Value*	placevalue.pdf placevalue.doc
172	Excerpt from *The Celebrated Jumping Frog of Calaveras County* by Mark Twain	jumpingfrog.pdf jumpingfrog.doc
175	*Early American Indians in the Southwestern United States*	earlyamerican.pdf earlyamerican.doc
178	Excerpt from *Macbeth* by William Shakespeare, Act I, Scene VII	macbeth.pdf macbeth.doc
180	*Our Wondrous Solar System*	solarsystem.pdf solarsystem.doc
182	Excerpt from *Crime and Punishment,* Part I, Chapter I by Fyodor Dostoevsky	crimeandpunishment.pdf crimeandpunishment.doc
185	Excerpt from *The Byzantine Empire: A Society that Shaped the World* by Kelly Rodgers from Byzantine Empire	byzantine.pdf byzantine.doc

Contents of Digital Resource CD (cont.)

Page	Title	Filename
195	*I Don't Want To…*	dontwantto.pdf dontwantto.doc
197	*Ice Cream Sundaes*	icecreamsundaes.pdf icecreamsundaes.doc
199	Excerpt from *My Father's Dragon* by Ruth Stiles Gannett	dragon.pdf dragon.doc
202	*Inside Land Biomes*	biomes.pdf biomes.doc
205	Excerpt from *King Lear,* Act I, Scene I, by William Shakespeare	kinglear.pdf kinglear.doc
208	*Corps of Discovery*	corpsdiscovery.pdf corpsdiscovery.doc
210	Excerpt from *The Heart of Darkness* by Joseph Conrad	heartdarkness.pdf heartdarkness.doc
212	*Rotations in Geometry*	rotations.pdf rotations.doc
214	Excerpt from *Frankenstein, or the Modern Prometheus* by Mary Wollstonecraft Shelley	frankenstein.pdf frankenstein.doc
217	Excerpt from *Women and War Work* by Helen Fraser	womenandwarwork.pdf womenandwarwork.doc
226	*Bears*	bears.pdf bears.doc
228	Excerpt from *Amazing Americans: Susan B. Anthony* by Stephanie Kuligowski	amazingamericans.pdf amazingamericans.doc
230	*Life in Colonial America*	lifecolonialamerica.pdf lifecolonialamerica.doc
233	Excerpt from *Jane Goodall: Animal Scientist and Friend* by Connie Jankowski	janegoodall.pdf janegoodall.doc
235	Excerpt from *The Declaration of Independence of the United States of America*	declaration.pdf declaration.doc
246	*Getting Around School*	school.pdf school.doc
247	*Follow That Map!*	map.pdf map.doc

Contents of Digital Resource CD (cont.)

Page	Title	Filename
250	*Little Red Riding-Hood* from *Old-time Stories, Fairy Tales and Myths Retold by Children* by E. Louise Smythe	littleredridinghood.pdf littleredridinghood.doc
253	*Little Red Riding Hood*	littleredridinghood1.pdf littleredridinghood1.doc
256	Excerpt from *Investigating Storms* by Debra J. Housel	storms.pdf storms.doc
257	Excerpt from *Inside the Water Cycle* by William B. Rice	watercycle.pdf watercycle.doc
259	"She Walks in Beauty" from *The Works of Lord Byron, Volume III* by Lord Byron	beauty.pdf beauty.doc
260	*Romeo and Juliet,* Act II, Scene II	romeojuliet.pdf romeojuliet.doc
262	*The Emancipation Proclamation* given by President Abraham Lincoln on September 22, 1862	emancipation.pdf emancipation.doc
264	Lincoln's *Gettysburg Address* given on November 19, 1863	gettysburg.pdf gettysburg.doc
265	Excerpt from Lincoln's *Second Inaugural Address* given March 4, 1865	inaugural.pdf inaugural.doc